Federated Learning

As data becomes more abundant and widespread across personal devices, the need for secure, privacy-aware machine learning is growing. Federated Learning (FL) offers a promising solution, enabling smart devices to collaboratively train models without sharing raw data. Yet, despite its benefits, FL faces serious risks from poisoning and inference attacks.

This book begins by introducing the fundamentals of machine learning, along with core deep learning architectures. Based on this foundation, it introduces the concept of Federated Learning (FL), which is a decentralised approach that enables collaborative model training without sharing raw data. The book provides an in-depth exploration of FL's various forms, system architectures, and practical applications. A significant emphasis is placed on the growing security and privacy concerns in FL, particularly poisoning (both data poisoning and model poisoning) and inference attacks. It discusses state-of-the-art mitigation strategies, such as Byzantine-robust aggregation and inference-resistant techniques, supported with practical implementation insights.

This book uniquely bridges foundational concepts with advanced topics in Federated Learning, offering a comprehensive view of its vulnerabilities and their mitigation. By combining theory with practical implementation of attacks and mitigation techniques, it serves as a valuable resource for researchers, practitioners, and students aiming to build secure, privacy-preserving collaborative machine learning systems.

This book is unique due to its end-to-end coverage of Federated Learning (FL), from foundational machine and deep learning concepts to real-time deployment of FL along with security and privacy challenges associated. It both explains theory and offers hands-on implementation of attacks and defenses. This practical approach, combined with a clear structure and real-world relevance, makes it ideal for both academic and industry audiences. Promotional emphasis should highlight the book's focus on actionable insights, its relevance to privacy-preserving and secure AI, and its utility as a learning and reference tool for building secure collaborative learning systems.

Federated Learning
Security and Privacy

Somanath Tripathy
Harsh Kasyap
Minghong Fang

CRC CRC Press
Taylor & Francis Group
Boca Raton New York London

CRC Press is an imprint of the
Taylor & Francis Group, an **informa** business

First edition published 2026
by CRC Press
2385 NW Executive Center Drive, Suite 320, Boca Raton FL 33431

and by CRC Press
4 Park Square, Milton Park, Abingdon, Oxon, OX14 4RN

CRC Press is an imprint of Taylor & Francis Group, LLC

© 2026 Somanath Tripathy, Harsh Kasyap and Minghong Fang

ISBN: 978-1-041-17462-2 (hbk)
ISBN: 978-1-041-17219-2 (pbk)
ISBN: 978-1-003-68857-0 (ebk)

DOI: 10.1201/9781003688570

Typeset in LMRoman
by SPi Technologies India Pvt Ltd (Straive)

To the glory of God,
Who inspired us to write this book and
brought it to completion

Contents

Preface

OVER THE PAST DECADE, MACHINE LEARNING HAS evolved as a critical enabler of modern intelligent systems. These systems pervade sensitive domains from healthcare and finance to mobile and smart environments. Now, the question of who owns the data and how it is used has become more important than ever. Federated Learning (FL) emerged as a promising answer, which is a decentralized, collaborative learning without moving the data out of the organization's premises. However, a new class of security and privacy risks still remains that is much more complex and nuanced than those in traditional machine learning. This book is motivated by a growing need for trustworthy federated learning systems. In particular, it focuses on what can go wrong and how to make it right. While FL seeks to preserve privacy by design, it is still not immune to adversarial, integrity, and privacy threats. Thus, malicious participants can poison training, manipulate model updates, or infer private data. At the same time, ensuring privacy can degrade model utility if not carefully balanced. Understanding this tradeoff and building practically secure FL systems are at the core of this book.

The book starts by laying the foundational concepts of machine learning, followed by a structured introduction to federated learning and its motivations, taxonomy, and key challenges. Subsequent chapters cover poisoning attacks, inference threats, and corresponding Byzantine-robust and privacy-preserving defenses. The focus is technical, with a strong emphasis on attack goals, implementation details, and critical evaluation of existing methods. Every chapter includes concrete algorithms and case studies to provide hands-on understanding. This structure will benefit both early-career researchers and practitioners who are working in the intersection of FL security and privacy.

This work is deeply informed by our own research over the years examining vulnerabilities in FL, designing adaptive attack strategies, and building countermeasures that work in real-world distributed environments. We hope readers find the material not only instructive but also thought-provoking and that it inspires further research.

Somanath Tripathy
Harsh Kasyap
Minghong Fang

Author Bios

Somanath Tripathy received his PhD from IIT Guwahati in 2007. Currently, he is a Professor in the Department of Computer Science and Engineering at the Indian Institute of Technology, Patna, where he has been a faculty member since December 2008. Prof. Tripathy has held significant administrative positions at IIT Patna, including Associate Dean of Academics (January 2016–March 2017), Head of the Computer Centre (November 2022–November 2023), and Associate Dean of Administration (July 2021–November 2023). His research interests encompass cybersecurity, malware detection, secure machine learning, lightweight cryptography, and blockchain. He holds two patents and has published over 130 research papers in reputed journals and conferences. He has led several projects as a Principal Investigator, notably his team developed a malware detection app presented to the Bureau of Police Research and Development (BPRD) and the Ministry of Home Affairs (MHA) as part of a sponsored project. He is currently an Editor of the *IETE Technical Review* and an Associate Editor of the journal *Multimedia Tools and Applications*.

Harsh Kasyap is an Assistant Professor in the Department of Computer Science and Engineering at the Indian Institute of Technology (BHU), Varanasi, India. He is also an Honorary Research Fellow at WMG, University of Warwick, UK. Prior to that, Harsh was a Research Associate at the Alan Turing Institute London, where he established significant research collaborations with HSBC, the Bank of Italy, and TNO, advancing the fields of data privacy, AI security, and fairness. He obtained his Ph.D. from IIT Patna, India. His Ph.D. thesis title was "Security and Privacy Preserving Techniques for Federated Learning". His research interests are federated learning, machine learning security, trustworthy AI, privacy, and data security.

Minghong Fang is a tenure-track Assistant Professor in the Department of Computer Science and Engineering at the University of Louisville. He was a Postdoctoral Associate in the Department of Electrical and Computer Engineering at Duke University from 2022 to 2024. He received his Ph.D. degree from the Department of Electrical and Computer Engineering at The Ohio State University in August 2022. He has published several high-impact research papers in top-tier security conferences, including the USENIX Security Symposium, the ACM Conference on Computer and Communications Security (CCS), and the Network and Distributed System Security (NDSS) Symposium. Notably, his USENIX Security 2020 paper was selected as one of the "Normalized Top-100 Security Papers Since 1981". His research interests broadly span various aspects of AI safety and security.

## CHAPTER 1

Introduction to Machine Learning

MACHINE LEARNING (ML) PROVIDES the ability to learn without being explicitly programmed. ML learns from experience (E) with respect to some tasks (T) and some performance measures (P). ML is centered around creating algorithms and models that enable systems to learn from data and subsequently make predictions or decisions. These algorithms employ statistical methods to autonomously enhance performance when encountering unseen data [81].

1.1 TYPES OF LEARNING

Machine Learning can broadly be classified based on data availability and learning process as Supervised, Unsupervised, and Reinforcement Learning [57].

Supervised Learning: This learning mechanism operates with labeled data, meaning a pair of input-output samples exists for learning. It aims to find a relationship between input and output and trains an algorithm to make predictions (regression) or classification tasks.

Unsupervised Learning: This learning mechanism operates with unlabeled data. It finds patterns or relationships within the data without any output label. Such learning techniques perform clustering tasks like finding similar customer groups for marketing analysis, i.e., reducing the dimensionality of data for visualization.

Reinforcement Learning: This learning technique works on coaching agents to navigate a series of choices within an environment to maximize the total rewards they accumulate. These agents acquire knowledge through trial and error, obtaining feedback from the environment regarding the consequences of their decisions. For example, training a robot to navigate a maze or teaching an AI to play a game like chess.

1.2 LEARNING TASKS

ML can also be broadly classified as regression and classification tasks [57].

Regression Tasks: Regression tasks aim to forecast a continuous numerical outcome as the prediction. The objective is establishing a pattern between input characteristics and the target parameter. For example, it includes predictions about real estate values, temperature fluctuations, financial stock rates, or an individual's age, all guided by various attributes. Frequently employed regression techniques encompass linear regression and support vector regression.

Classification Tasks: Classification tasks involve predicting a categorical label or class as the prediction. In such scenarios, the aim is to allocate input data points to predetermined groups or classes. For example, it includes tasks like

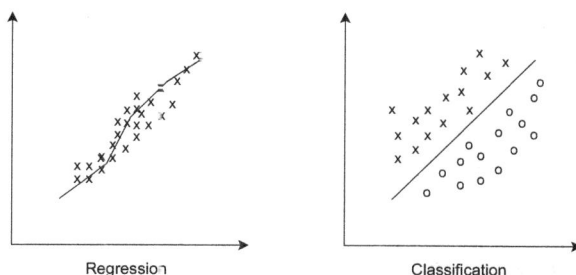

Regression   Classification

FIGURE 1.1   Regression and classification.

classifying images to recognize objects, identifying spam or legitimate emails, making medical diagnoses based on patient information to ascertain the existence or absence of disease, and identifying a class of network threat. Frequently employed classification techniques encompass logistic regression, decision trees, random forests, support vector machines, and neural networks.

As shown in Figure 1.1, regression tasks aim to predict continuous values, while classification tasks aim to categorize into a discrete label or class.

1.3 COST FUNCTION

Assume we have a private dataset with input features (often denoted as X) and corresponding output labels (often denoted as Y), and we want to build a model that can predict the labels based on the input features. The cost function (denoted as J) quantifies the difference between the predicted ($f(X)$) and actual output values (Y). It calculates how wrong the model makes the predictions and is denoted as $J(f(X), Y)$. The cost function depends on the particular problem and may change based on the requirement (type of ML tasks). For example, standard cost functions include Mean Squared Error (MSE) for regression problems and Cross-Entropy Loss for classification problems.

Mean Squared Error: While working with regression tasks, the Mean Squared Error (MSE) is the typical cost function, as stated below.

$$J(f(X), Y) = \frac{1}{n} \sum_{i=1}^{n} (f(X_i) - Y_i)^2, \tag{1.1}$$

where n is the total number of data samples, X_i is the ith input data, Y_i is the corresponding (actual) target value, and $f(X_i)$ is the predicted target value.

Cross-Entropy Loss: While working with classification tasks, the Cross-Entropy Loss (also known as Log Loss) is the typical cost function, as stated below:

$$J(f(X), Y) = -\frac{1}{n} \sum_{i=1}^{n} (Y_i \cdot \log(f(X_i))$$
$$+ (1 - Y_i) \cdot \log(1 - f(X_i))), \tag{1.2}$$

where n is the total number of data samples, X_i is the ith input data, Y_i is the corresponding (actual) target class label, and $f(X_i)$ is the predicted target class label.

1.4 OPTIMIZATION

Machine learning models are optimized to minimize the cost function and find the best model parameters. Gradient descent is an optimization algorithm that runs iteratively to adjust the parameters. It computes the gradients of cost function with respect to each parameter. The gradient reveals the direction and magnitude of the steep increase in the cost function.

Then, the parameters are updated by subtracting a fraction (the learning rate (α)) of the gradients from their current values. The learning rate (α) determines the step size of the parameter update.

Mathematically, a parameter θ_j is updated as follows:

$$\theta_j := \theta_j - \alpha \cdot \frac{\partial J}{\partial \theta_j}, \qquad (1.3)$$

where $\frac{\partial J}{\partial \theta_j}$ is the partial derivative of the cost function w.r.t. θ_j, which represents the change in cost function due to θ_j.

Gradient descent can be computed differently, for example, Batch Gradient Descent, Stochastic Gradient Descent, and Mini-Batch Gradient Descent.

There is a bias-variance tradeoff issue, discovered in ML. This causes two different issues, called underfitting and overfitting of the model.

1.4.1 Underfitting

Underfitting represents high bias. It causes both high training and testing errors. It mostly happens due to fewer features available for training. As shown in Figure 1.2, in the case of underfitting, the model does not learn enough to classify even the training samples.

1.4.2 Overfitting

Overfitting represents high variance. It causes low training errors but high testing errors. It is due to training with

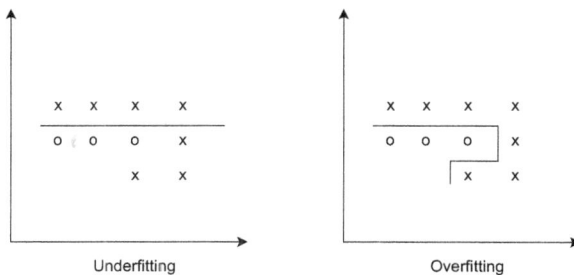

FIGURE 1.2   Underfitting and overfitting.

more features. In the case of overfitting, the model is trained extensively to do well on the training samples, as shown in Figure 1.2. Thus, it makes the model perform worse on unseen data. Overfitting is a significant problem, as the model often overfits the training data.

It is a better practice to select essential features to train the model. Otherwise, regularization needs to be used while training.

1.4.3 Regularization

Regularization increases the model generalized by adding a regularization term to the cost function. It keeps the parameters within certain bounds by adding a penalty to the cost function. It makes the model balance fitting training data and keeping parameters within bounds.

Mathematically, the regularized cost function is written as follows:

$$J_{\text{regularized}} = J + \text{regularization\_term}. \qquad (1.4)$$

The most common regularization terms are L1 (Lasso) and L2 (Ridge) regularization.

L1 regularization: It sums up the absolute values of the parameters as $\lambda \sum_{i=1}^{n} |\theta_i|$ to the cost function. Here λ is the constant determining the tradeoff between the learning (fitting) over the training data and model complexity, and θ_i are the model's parameters.

L2 regularization: It sums up the squared values of the parameters as $\lambda \sum_{i=1}^{n} |\theta_i^2|$ to the cost function. Here λ is the constant determining the tradeoff between the learning (fitting) over the training data and model complexity, and θ_i are the model's parameters.

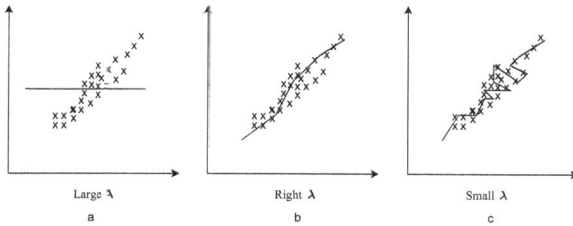

FIGURE 1.3   Regularization effects.

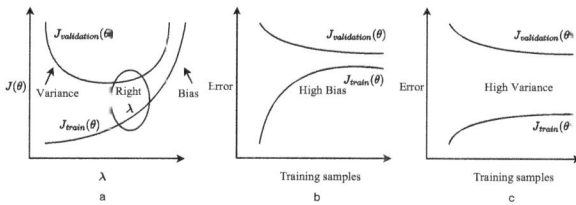

FIGURE 1.4   Regularization and cost effects.

A large value of λ would increase the regularization effect, resulting in underfitting. Figure 1.3 illustrates the impact of choosing different λ. Figure 1.4a demonstrates how training and validation errors get affected by λ and the number of training samples. It can be seen that a lower λ causes high variance, where the model performs well on training data but very poorly on the validation data. On the other hand, a higher λ value causes high bias, where the model performs poorly on both the training and validation data. Figure 1.4b and 1.4c show how the relationship between the number of training samples and error causes high bias and variance.

1.5 EVALUATION METRICS

The following evaluation metrics are primarily used to test the different machine learning models.

1.5.1 Regression Metrics

1. *Mean Squared Error (MSE):* MSE is the average-squared difference between the true and predicted values, i.e.,

$$\text{MSE} = \frac{1}{n} \sum_{i=1}^{n} (Y_i - \hat{Y}_i)^2, \qquad (1.5)$$

where n is the total number of data points, Y_i is the true value, and $\hat{Y}_i$ is the predicted value of ith data point.

A lower MSE value indicates better performance for the model. It is susceptible to the outliers.

2. *Root Mean Squared Error (RMSE)*: RMSE is an extension to MSE, which is the square root of the average squared difference between the true and predicted values. It is defined as follows:

$$\text{RMSE} = \sqrt{\frac{1}{n} \sum_{i=1}^{n} (Y_i - \hat{Y}_i)^2}, \qquad (1.6)$$

where n is the total number of data points, Y_i is the true value, and $\hat{Y}_i$ is the predicted value of ith data point.

Similarly, a low RMSE indicates a better performance of the model. It is also sensitive to the outliers. RMSE may be used more often because it is measured in the same units.

3. *Mean Absolute Error (MAE):* MAE is the absolute difference between true and predicted values; it can be written as follows:

$$\text{MAE} = \frac{1}{n} \sum_{i=1}^{n} |Y_i - \hat{Y}_i|, \qquad (1.7)$$

where n is the total number of data points, Y_i is the true value, and $\hat{Y}_i$ is the predicted value of ith data point.

Like other metrics, a low MAE indicates a better model performance. It is less sensitive to outliers because it gives equal weight to all the values and treats all the errors equally.

1.5.2 Classification Metrics

1. *Accuracy:* It measures the proportion of correctly predicted samples to the total number of samples. It can be stated as follows:

$$\text{Accuracy} = \frac{\text{Correctly classified samples}}{\text{Total number of samples}} \quad (1.8)$$

It is suitable when the samples are uniform (balanced) across all classes in the classification task. Otherwise, there could still be high accuracy if the model correctly predicted the majority class. Also, it doesn't provide an analysis of critical and non-critical cases.

2. *Precision:* Precision measures the proportion of all correctly predicted positive samples to total predicted positive samples in the dataset. It is also written as:

$$\text{Precision} = \frac{\text{True Positives}}{\text{True Positives} + \text{False Positives}}, \quad (1.9)$$

where True Positives (TP) are correctly predicted positive samples and False Positives (FP) are samples predicted positive but actually negative. It is useful when working with imbalanced classes.

3. *Recall:* Recall measures the proportion of all correctly predicted positive samples to total actual positive samples in the dataset. It can be written as:

$$\text{Recall} = \frac{\text{True Positives}}{\text{True Positives} + \text{False Negatives}}, \quad (1.10)$$

where True Positives (TP) are correctly predicted positive samples and False Negatives (FN) are samples predicted negative but actually positive. It is also useful when working with imbalanced classes.

The recall is very significant, when safety is paramount. Thus, maximizing the identification of positive samples is more important. Meanwhile, minimizing the risk of false positive predictions in precision is more important.

4. *F1-Score:* It measures the performance of the model, considering both precision and recall. It can be written as:

$$\text{F1-score} = 2 \times \frac{\text{Precision} \times \text{Recall}}{\text{Precision} + \text{Recall}}. \qquad (1.11)$$

This is very useful for imbalanced datasets. Moreover, it balances both precision and recall. It is lower when either precision or recall is low.

5. *Confusion Matrix:* It is a tabular representation summarizing the model's performance by showing the counts of true positive (TP), true negative (TN), false positive (FP), and false negative (FN) predictions. The confusion matrix provides a comprehensive view of the performance of the model.

1.5.3 Clustering Metrics

1. *Silhouette Score:* It measures cluster's quality in an unsupervised machine learning model. It finds how well-separated the clusters are from each other, including the assignment of data samples to correct labels. It lies in the range of -1 to 1. It is also written as:

$$s(i) = \frac{b(i) - a(i)}{max\{a(i), b(i)\}}, \qquad (1.12)$$

where $a(i)$ is the average distance of ith sample to other samples in the same cluster and $b(i)$ is the smallest among the average distance of ith sample to other samples in different clusters.

A high score means the samples inside a cluster are tightly packed and well-separated from other clusters, while a negative cluster means samples might have been wrongly clustered. However, choosing the number of clusters remains the problem. A high Silhouette Score does not guarantee this. Also, it works well, assuming clusters are convex and have the same sizes.

2. *Davies-Bouldin Index:* This index helps determine the number of clusters and evaluate the clusters' separation and compactness. It is measured as the average similarity between each cluster and its most similar cluster. It is also written as:

$$DB(C_i) = \frac{1}{n_i \sum_{j=1, j \neq i}^{k} R_{ij}}, \qquad (1.13)$$

where n_i is the number of samples in C_i and R_{ij} is the dissimilarity measure between C_i and C_j. It is defined as the sum of distances between samples, normalized by some measure of the spread, in clusters i and j. Then, the overall Davies-Bouldin Index is the maximum of the Davies-Bouldin Index over all clusters.

A lower Davies-Bouldin Index means better-defined and well-separated clusters. Like the Silhouette Score, it works well, assuming clusters are convex and have the same sizes.

3. *Dunn Index:* It also determines the separation and compactness of clusters by measuring the ratio of minimum inter-cluster distance to the maximum intra-cluster

distance. It quantifies both the separation between clusters and spread within clusters. It is also written as:

$$\mathrm{DI} = \frac{\min_{i \neq j}(\text{inter-cluster distance})}{\max_i(\text{intra-cluster distance})}, \qquad (1.14)$$

where the inter-cluster distance between clusters i and j is calculated between their centroids, and the intra-cluster distance is the average of maximum distance between samples within the cluster.

A higher Dunn Index means better-defined and well-separated clusters.

1.6 ARTIFICIAL NEURAL NETWORK

An artificial neural network (ANN) consists of interconnected nodes known as neurons. Neurons are grouped into layers: input layers, hidden layers, and output layers. As information flows through the network, it starts at the input layer, passes through the hidden layers, and finally reaches the output layer. Weighted inputs are processed by each neuron in the network, and activation functions are applied to produce outputs for the next layer. Activation functions introduce nonlinearity into the network, allowing it to learn complex relationships from data using weighted inputs. An ANN with multiple hidden layers is called a deep neural network (DNN).

Figure 1.5 illustrates an artificial neural network, with an input layer having three neurons, a hidden layer with four neurons, and an output layer representing the number of classes, i.e., 2. By adjusting the weights of its connections, an ANN minimizes the difference between its predicted and actual outputs. The above-discussed gradient descent is used as an algorithm to solve this optimization problem. This learning process can be discussed in two passes: forward and

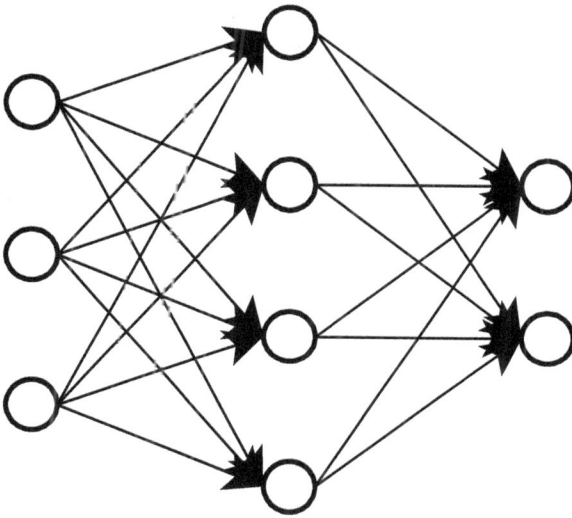

FIGURE 1.5   Artificial Neural Network.

backward pass. In the forward pass, input data propagates through the network to generate predictions. It can also be written as follows:

$$z = \sum_{i=1}^{n} (w_i \cdot x_i) + b, \qquad (1.15)$$

where for a single neuron in a layer, the output (z) is calculated as the weighted sum ($w_i \cdot x_i$), where w_i are the weights and input x_i supplied from the previous layer, with a bias b (to shift the activation function). Then, an activation function is applied to each neuron's output, i.e., $a(z)$, and passed to the next layer. Next, using a loss function, the network performance is measured. Then, backpropagation calculates the gradient of the loss with regard to the weights, which indicates how much weight should be adjusted to reduce the loss. Gradient descent is used to update the weights. This process is repeated until the loss is minimized.

1.6.1 Convolutional Neural Network

A Convolutional Neural Network (CNN) is a type of neural network that is primarily used for learning with image and classification tasks. Throughout this book, most of the examples are discussed with reference to images and CNN-based models.

CNN has three components: convolutional, pooling, and fully connected (FC) layers. Thus, CNN is an extension of a simple neural network. This is because the images are large, and it would increase the number of parameters in a simple neural network. Thus, CNN encodes images using the convolutional and pooling layer into meaningful features, which becomes easier to capture by the forward layer. For example, an image of size $(300 \times 300 \times 3)$ would lead to $300 \times 300 \times 300 = 270,000$ weights. Thus, defining a simple neuron network with 270,000 weights as input is almost infeasible. Therefore, to overcome this, CNN also works in layers. For example, for the above image, CNN will also have neurons in three dimensions.

The convolutional layer transforms the input images by performing convolution with a small matrix called the kernel. It performs a dot product between the input matrix and the kernel. The kernel slides the complete input matrix. If the input image size is $W \times W \times D$, the size of the kernel matrix is K, the sliding size (stride) is S, and the padding required in images is P; then the output comes to $W_C = \frac{W-K+2P}{S}$. For N kernels, the output comes to $W_C \times W_C \times N$. Then, activation can be applied element-wise. Pooling layer is a downsampling operation, which reduces $W_C \times W_C \times N$ to $W_c \times W_c \times N$, where $c < C$. Finally, the FC layer takes $W_c \times W_c \times N$ as input and outputs the final scores for each class.

1.7 IMPLEMENTATION

The implementation of a simple CNN for the classification task of MNIST and Fashion-MNIST images is given below.

1.7.1 CNN Model

```python
class ModelMNIST(nn.Module):
    def __init__(self):
        super(ModelMNIST, self).__init__()
        self.conv1 = nn.Conv2d(1, 32, 3, 1)
        self.conv2 = nn.Conv2d(32, 64, 3, 1)
        self.dropout1 = nn.Dropout2d(0.25)
        self.dropout2 = nn.Dropout2d(0.5)
        self.fc1 = nn.Linear(9216, 128)
        self.fc2 = nn.Linear(128, 10)
        self.softmax = nn.Softmax(dim=1)

    def forward(self, x):
        x = self.conv1(x)
        x = F.relu(x)
        x = self.conv2(x)
        x = F.relu(x)
        x = F.max_pool2d(x, 2)
        x = self.dropout1(x)
        x = torch.flatten(x, 1)
        x = self.fc1(x)
        x = F.relu(x)
        x = self.dropout2(x)
        x = self.fc2(x)
        output = self.softmax(x)
        return output
```

1.7.2 Training

```python
train_data = datasets.MNIST(root=datadir, train
    =True, transform=transforms.ToTensor(),
    download=True)
test_data = datasets.MNIST(root=datadir, train=
    False, transform=transforms.ToTensor(),
    download=True)
```

```
train_loader = torch.utils.data.DataLoader(
    train_data,batch_size=128, shuffle=True)
test_loader = torch.utils.data.DataLoader(
    test_data, batch_size=1000)

model.train()
train_loss = []
train_accu = []
i = 0

loss_fn = torch.nn.CrossEntropyLoss()
for epoch in range(5):
    for data, target in train_loader:
        data, target = Variable(data), Variable
            (target)
        optimizer.zero_grad()
        output = model(data)
        loss= loss_fn(output, target)
        loss.backward()      # calc gradients
        train_loss.append(loss.item())
        optimizer.step()   # update gradients
        prediction = output.data.max(1)[1]     #
            first column has actual prob.
        accuracy = prediction.eq(target.data).
            sum()/batch_size*100
        train_accu.append(accuracy)
        if i % 1000 == 0:
            print('Train Step: {}\tLoss: {:.3f
                }\tAccuracy: {:.3f}'.format(i,
                loss.item(), accuracy))
        i += 1
```

1.7.3 Evaluation

```
model.eval()
correct = 0
for data, target in test_loader:
    data, target = Variable(data, volatile=True
        ), Variable(target)
    output = model(data)
```

```
6    loss = F.nll_loss(output, target)
7    prediction = output.data.max(1)[1]
8    correct += prediction.eq(target.data).sum()
9
10 print('\nTest set: \tLoss: {:.3f}\tAccuracy:
       {:.3f}'.format(loss, 100. * correct / len(
       test_loader.dataset)))
```

## CHAPTER 2

Federated Learning

FEDERATED LEARNING (FL) [50, 51] is a decentralized machine learning approach that allows organizations and individuals to train machine learning models on the data that are distributed across multiple devices or nodes without the need to transfer the data to a central server. FL enables data privacy by keeping the data locally and only sending model updates back and forth between the devices and the central server. The central server aggregates the model updates from the devices, and the aggregated model is then used for inference or further training.

2.1 DEFINITION OF FL

In Vanilla FL, the central server (CS) initiates the process, and other participants could be a smartphone, laptop, or any other computing device that can participate in the FL process. In each iteration of the FL process, CS sends the current global model to each device. Each device then uses its local dataset to compute the local model update, which is returned to CS. Then, CS aggregates the local model updates to produce a new global model, which will be sent back to all devices for

DOI: 10.1201/9781003688570-2

the next iteration. This process continues until convergence is reached or a stopping criterion is met.

FL is mathematically described as an optimization problem that aims to minimize a global loss function over a distributed dataset. Let us consider a set of (m) devices, denoted by $D = \{D_1, D_2, \dots, D_m\}$, each with its own local dataset, denoted by $X_1, X_2, \dots, X_m$. Each device has access to a local model, denoted by w_i, where $i = 1, 2, \dots, m$.

The objective of FL is to train a global model, denoted by w, by aggregating the local models of the devices. The global model is updated iteratively using a centralized server, denoted by CS. At each iteration t, each device D_i computes a local model update, denoted by $\triangle w_i^t$, by minimizing its own local loss function, denoted by $L_i(w_i; X_i)$. This can be expressed mathematically as follows:

$$\triangle w_i^t = argmin_{w_i} L_i(w_i; X_i). \tag{2.1}$$

Each local model update is then sent to the central server S, aggregating them to produce the new global model w^{t+1}. The aggregation function can be a simple-weighted average, as denoted by Equation 2.2:

$$w^{t+1} = \sum_{i=1}^{m} p_i \triangle w_i^t, \tag{2.2}$$

where p_i is the weight assigned to the device D_i.

The global model w^{t+1} is then sent back to all the devices, where it is used to update their local models for the next iteration. This process is repeated until convergence, or a stopping criterion, is met.

FL can also incorporate regularization techniques, such as L1 or L2 regularization to prevent overfitting of the local model. This can be expressed mathematically as stated in Equation 2.3:

$$\triangle w_i^t = argmin_{w_i} L_i(w_i; X_i) + \lambda \|w_i\|_p, \qquad (2.3)$$

where λ is the regularization parameter and $\|w_i\|_p$ is the p-norm of the weight vector w_i.

FL has several advantages over traditional machine learning methods. The primary advantage of FL is its ability to preserve data privacy, as data is never sent to the central server. This ensures that sensitive data remains secure and private. Another advantage of FL is its ability to scale to large datasets. By training locally on devices, FL can handle datasets that are too large to be stored on a central server. Furthermore, FL can handle real-time data by training locally on devices and transmitting the updates to the central server, reducing the latency associated with traditional machine learning methods. Above all, FL facilitates collaboration across different organizations, enabling knowledge sharing while preserving data privacy.

2.2 IMPORTANCE OF FL

FL is an important approach that allows models to be trained using data distributed across multiple devices or servers. Following are some of the main reasons for its popularity.

- *Privacy:* One of the main advantages of FL is that it protects the privacy of users' data. With FL, data is kept on users' devices and is never shared directly with the central server. This is indispensable for applications that involve sensitive data, such as healthcare or finance.

- *Efficiency:* FL is much more efficient than traditional machine learning approaches that require all data to be centralized. With FL, computation is distributed across multiple devices, thus reducing the time and resources needed for training.

- *Scalability:* FL is very scalable, as it allows models to be trained using data from many devices or servers. So, it is useful for applications that require large amounts of data to be processed, such as social networks or e-commerce platforms.

- *Data Access:* FL allows models to be trained using data from a diverse range of sources, including devices not typically connected to the internet or in areas with limited connectivity. This can help increase the amount of data available for training and improve the accuracy of the models.

- *Robustness:* FL can also be more robust than traditional machine learning approaches, as it allows models to be trained using data from diverse sources. So, it prevents overfitting and improves the generalization performance of the model.

- *Regulatory Compliance:* FL would facilitate organizations to comply with regulations that restrict the sharing or storage of data, such as the Digital Personal Data Protection Bill (DPDPB) in India and General Data Protection Regulation (GDPR [17]) in the European Union.

Overall, FL can address many challenges associated with traditional machine learning approaches, including privacy, efficiency, data access, scalability, robustness, and regulatory compliance, an indispensable technique for building a collaborative learning system.

2.3 TYPES OF FL

FL can be classified into different categories based on practical use cases, data composition, partition, and computing resources.

2.3.1 Cross-Device and Cross-Silo FL

Cross-device FL involves resource-constrained edge devices as participants. These devices may be intelligent devices, mobiles, laptops, IoT devices, etc. Edge devices own local data and train locally over it. However, it is almost impossible to do any computation over the local data due to the limited computation available. Google uses cross-device FL to train its next-word prediction model.

Cross-silo FL involves large (silo) organizations with computational resources. These organizations are like hospitals, schools, or companies that own large amounts of data and process their data. They train over the local data and share the trained local model with the central server. Figure 2.1 illustrates cross-device and cross-silo FL.

2.3.2 FL Based on Data Partitioning

FL can be categorized based on data partition across participants. This is based on feature and sample spaces. Features

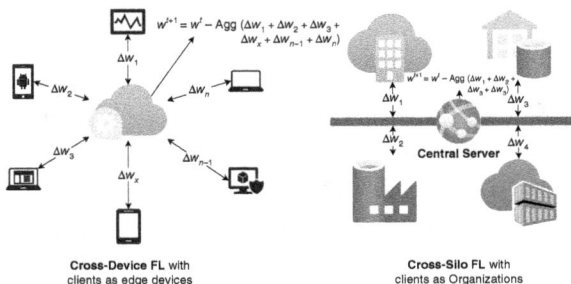

Cross-Device FL with clients as edge devices

Cross-Silo FL with clients as Organizations

FIGURE 2.1   FL schemes.

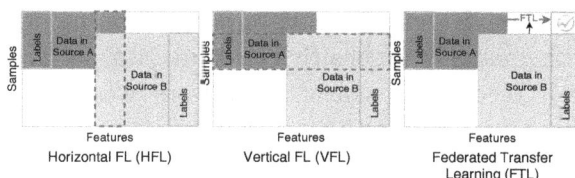

FIGURE 2.2 FL based on data partitioning.

represent the key attributes in a data sample, while a sample is a data bundle owned by any device.

Horizontal FL (HFL), also known as sample-based FL, represents shared feature space among the participants with different samples. In horizontal FL, participants have a homogeneous set of data. This form of FL is the most efficient (involves low communication costs) and fault-tolerant. It benefits from data divergence and deals with heterogeneity in sample space.

Vertical FL (VFL), also known as feature-based FL, involves shared sample space but different features among the participants. This sort of FL is used across big organizations working over a shared set of customers. Vertical FL incurs more computation and communication costs to ensure privacy and model training.

Federated Transfer Learning (FTL) integrates HFL and VFL. FTL includes transferring knowledge across domains with different features and sample space. In FTL, the model is trained for a particular application and then applied (transferred) to a separate application within a similar domain. The model depends on the domain of various problems being similar. Figure 2.2 illustrates FL based on data partitioning.

2.4 APPLICATIONS OF FL

FL has numerous applications in various fields, some of them are enumerated below.

1. *Healthcare:* FL enables collaborative training of machine learning models on sensitive medical data, such as patient health records or sensor data from wearable devices, without transferring the raw data to a central server. This approach preserves patient privacy while supporting predictive healthcare and personalized treatment models [27, 39]. This approach can be very helpful in clinical research and drug discovery. Being a very sensitive domain, it is strictly prohibited to share raw data among the healthcare organizations, particularly in countries with very strict data sharing regulations such as GDPR and HIPPA.

2. *Internet of Things (IoT):* FL supports decentralized model training across a wide network of smart devices, including those in homes, factories, and cities. By keeping data on devices, FL reduces communication overhead and ensures privacy, making it suitable for applications such as energy optimization and behavioral analytics [54]. This enables us to design and develop smart applications, including smart cities, smart traffic management, smart home, and many more applications.

3. *Autonomous Vehicles:* FL allows multiple autonomous vehicles to collaboratively train models using locally collected data, such as traffic patterns, road conditions, and sensor inputs. This promotes safer and more adaptive driving systems without requiring vehicles to share raw data, thus preserving both privacy and proprietary information [38]. Connected autonomous vehicles (CAVs) have been studied as an interdisciplinary approach, where it requires a very real-time secure communication between sensors, fog (middleware layer), and the central coordinating server.

4. *Financial Services:* In the financial domain, FL can be used to train fraud detection or credit risk models

using models trained on sensitive data from multiple financial institutions. The data remains on the institution premises, ensuring compliance with data protection regulations [45]. This can help remove biases in lending across demographics. Since it has been observed that there exists inherent bias in the local dataset due to issues such as sample or labeling bias. FL can be very helpful to mitigate the bias across the institutions.

5. *Natural Language Processing (NLP):* FL facilitates model training on user-generated text data, such as chat messages or typing patterns, across distributed devices. This supports applications like predictive text or sentiment analysis while safeguarding users' local data and communication privacy [29]. It can be particularly useful in detecting and mitigating hateful contents on social sites.

6. *Federated Image Recognition:* FL enables the training of image recognition models using photos or visual inputs from users' smartphones, surveillance systems, or other edge devices. By keeping the image data local, FL avoids privacy breaches while supporting applications like facial recognition and object detection [80].

7. *Anomaly Detection:* FL is well-suited for training anomaly detection models across data from different organizations or systems. This is particularly useful in cybersecurity, where FL can help detect malware or network intrusions without requiring centralized access to sensitive logs or system traces [62].

2.5 CHALLENGES IN FL

While FL has shown great promise in overcoming the limitations of traditional centralized machine learning, there are still several challenges associated with this technique.

- *Heterogeneity of Devices:* FL requires a diverse range of devices to participate in the learning process, often resulting in heterogeneity in hardware, operating systems, and network connectivity. Therefore, it is challenging to standardize the learning process and ensure that all devices can effectively participate in the training process.

- *Privacy Concerns:* FL requires that devices share their local models with the central server for aggregation, which raises concerns about the privacy and security of sensitive user data. There is a risk that individual data points or patterns may be revealed by the model updates sent to the server, which could limit the adoption of FL.

- *Communication Overhead:* FL requires significant communication between devices and the central server, which results in slow training times, high network latency, and potential bottlenecks in the communication process.

- *Federated Optimization:* The aggregation of local model updates is a complex optimization problem requiring careful tuning of aggregation algorithms and hyperparameters. This is challenging, particularly in scenarios with high heterogeneity among devices or when data is distributed unevenly across devices.

- *Bias and Fairness:* FL relies on a representative sample of devices to participate in the learning process, leading to selection bias and unfairness. This can result in models skewed toward specific demographics or groups, negatively affecting the learning process's accuracy and fairness.

2.6 SECURITY AND PRIVACY ISSUES IN FL

FL has emerged as a promising approach to collaborative machine learning. However, the decentralized nature of FL raises significant security and privacy concerns that must be addressed to ensure the safety and trustworthiness of the approach.

One of the primary security concerns in FL is the risk of malicious attacks or data breaches. Since FL relies on the aggregation of local model updates from multiple devices, there is a risk that an attacker could compromise one or more devices to inject false or misleading updates into the learning process [8, 20, 26]. This could undermine the learning process's accuracy and fairness and compromise user data's security and privacy. Another significant concern in FL is the privacy of user data [46, 61]. As FL relies on the participation of multiple devices, there is a risk that sensitive user data is exposed or compromised during the learning process. This could undermine user trust and limit the adoption of FL in scenarios where privacy is a concern.

Apart from that, some ethical and regulatory considerations are also associated with FL. For example, using FL in healthcare or finance requires compliance with regulations such as HIPAA, GDPR, and DPDPB, which place strict requirements on collecting, storing, and processing sensitive user data. Similarly, the use of FL in scenarios such as hiring or lending may raise concerns about bias and fairness, as the learning process may inadvertently discriminate against certain groups or demographics.

2.6.1 Poisoning Attacks

In a poisoning attack, an attacker aims to inject malicious data or updates into the learning process to compromise the integrity of the global model. Such attacks undermine the accuracy and effectiveness of an FL model.

There are several ways in which poisoning attacks can be carried out in FL. One common approach is to compromise one or more devices and inject false or misleading updates into the local models. These updates may be designed to bias the learning process toward a specific outcome or undermine the global model's accuracy and stability. Another approach is manipulating data distribution across devices so that particular devices are overrepresented or underrepresented in the learning process. This can result in models skewed toward certain groups or demographics, negatively affecting the learning process's accuracy and fairness.

In FL, different types of poisoning attacks can be crafted by malicious clients to manipulate the global model's learning process. Following are some common types of poisoning attacks in FL:

- *Label-flipping attack:* In a label-flipping attack, the attacker modifies the labels of some of their local data samples to degrade the performance of the global model [78]. For example, the attacker may swap the labels of two data classes, making it difficult for the global model to classify those classes accurately.

- *Data poisoning attack:* In a data poisoning attack, the attacker injects incorrect or malicious data into their local dataset to influence the global model's learning process [4]. The attacker's objective is to compromise the integrity of the global model and affect its accuracy.

- *Model poisoning attack:* In a model poisoning attack, the attacker modifies the local model before sending it to the server for aggregation [6, 18, 60]. The attacker may introduce a backdoor in the local model that can be triggered later to compromise the global model's accuracy.

- *Byzantine attack:* In a Byzantine attack, the attacker behaves maliciously by sending incorrect or random model updates to the server during the training process. The attacker's objective is to disrupt the learning process of the global model, leading to incorrect predictions [21].

In FL, poisoning attacks can be categorized into two types: untargeted [7, 32] and targeted [4, 44].

An untargeted poisoning attack is an attack where a malicious client injects incorrect or malicious data into their local dataset without any specific objective. The attacker's goal is to compromise the model's overall accuracy, making it less useful for the intended purpose. On the other hand, a targeted poisoning attack is a type of attack where the attacker manipulates the local data to influence the learning process in a way that favors their objective. For example, in a classification task, the attacker targets to misclassify a specific class of data. Targeted poisoning attacks are typically more challenging to detect and mitigate than untargeted attacks, as the attacker carefully selects and crafts the poisoned data to degrade the accuracy of a specific class.

2.6.2 Inference Attacks

Inference attacks in FL refer to exploiting local models to gain insights into the local data used to train the model [31, 46, 61]. Such attacks allow an attacker to learn sensitive information about the client's data and thus fail to preserve the clients' privacy. For example, if the global model is trained on medical data, an attacker could use the model's output to infer sensitive information about the patients, like medical conditions and history, without having access to the client's data.

There are several types of inference attacks, including membership inference attacks [61], attribute inference attacks [46], and model inversion attacks [19, 31]. Such attacks are carried out by a malicious client who has access to the output of the global model and some knowledge of the distribution of the training data.

- *Membership Inference Attacks:* These attacks aim to determine whether a particular data sample was used in the training dataset of the model [61]. The attacker trains a classifier on a set of auxiliary data samples and then uses this classifier to predict whether a particular data sample was present in the training dataset. If the classifier's prediction is accurate, the attacker can infer that the data sample was used for training.

- *Attribute Inference Attacks:* The attribute inference attack aims to infer sensitive information about the training data, such as attributes or labels, by analyzing the global model outputs [46]. The attacker can use the output of the global model to infer sensitive information about the training data. For example, suppose the global model is trained on medical data. In that case, an attacker might try to infer whether a particular patient has a specific medical condition by analyzing the model's output.

- *Model Inversion Attacks:* Model inversion attacks aim to infer sensitive information about the training data by reverse engineering the global model [31]. The attacker can use the output of the worldwide model to infer information about the training data, such as features or labels. Using this information, the attacker can reverse engineer the global model to obtain a copy of the training data.

2.7 DEFENSE TECHNIQUES

Several defense techniques exist to resist poisoning and inference attacks in federated learning (FL).

2.7.1 Byzantine-Robust FL

Byzantine-robust FL aims to ensure the trained models are accurate and robust, even when some participants are malicious. A Byzantine robust FL requires a combination of techniques to protect the model's accuracy and performance in malicious device's presence. These techniques include model averaging, gradient clipping, robust aggregation, adaptive regularization, and Byzantine-resilient Stochastic Gradient Descent.

- *Model Averaging:* Model averaging [51] involves aggregating the model parameters from multiple devices to generate a single model. This approach reduces malicious behavior's impact, as a single device's contribution is limited.

- *Gradient Clipping:* Gradient clipping [11] is a simple approach that limits the magnitude of the gradients sent by the participating devices. This can help prevent malicious devices from sending large gradients that could distort the model.

- *Robust Aggregation:* Robust aggregation [3, 11, 41, 49, 74] techniques aim to detect and exclude malicious devices during the model aggregation, by using techniques such as Median-of-Means Aggregation or Secure Aggregation with Differential Privacy.

- *Adaptive Regularization:* Adaptive regularization [13] adjusts the regularization parameter during training based on the performance of the participating devices. This can help to prevent overfitting caused by malicious devices.

- *Byzantine-Resilient Stochastic Gradient Descent:* Byzantine-resilient Stochastic Gradient Descent (B-SGD) [71] uses a variant of stochastic gradient descent that is resilient to Byzantine failures. B-SGD protects the model's accuracy and performance even when some participating devices behave maliciously.

2.7.2 Inference-Resistant FL

Inference-resistant FL protects the privacy of sensitive information in training data by limiting the amount of sensitive information inferred from the global model. Following are the popular techniques used to build inference-resistant FL.

- *Differential Privacy (DP):* DP [16] is a technique that adds random noise to the model updates before they are aggregated. This randomization makes it more difficult for an attacker to infer sensitive information about the data, as the exact contribution of any one client cannot be determined with certainty. Thus, no individual user's data can be reconstructed from the model [68].

- *Secure Multi-Party Computation (SMPC):* SMPC [72] is a cryptographic technique that allows multiple parties to perform computations on their private data without revealing it to the other parties. SMPC can be used to ensure that the data remains encrypted during the computation process, thus preventing attackers from intercepting and reconstructing the data [28].

- *Homomorphic Encryption (HE):* HE [73] is a cryptographic technique that allows computations to be performed on encrypted data without the need for decryption. In FL, HE can be used to encrypt the model updates before they are sent to the central server to ensure that no participant's data is revealed during the computation process [77].

- *Federated Transfer Learning (FTL):* In FTL [43], pretrained models are used as a starting point for training on user data rather than starting from scratch. This approach can reduce the amount of data needed from each user, reducing the risk of inference attacks.

- *Ensembling:* Ensembling [42] is a technique that combines multiple models to improve accuracy and reduce the risk of overfitting. It can be used to integrate models from various users, which makes it difficult for attackers to infer participants' data.

- *Secure Function Evaluation (SFE):* SFE [59] is a cryptographic technique that allows multiple parties to jointly compute a function without revealing their inputs. SFE can compute the model updates without revealing any participant's data.

A tradeoff exists between robustness and privacy in the existing defense techniques. Existing Byzantine-robust defense techniques require raw (plaintext) access to the participant's local model updates. Thus, applying inference-resistant approaches restricts the execution of Byzantine-robust defenses and exposes FL to poisoning attacks. Therefore, it demands a privacy-preserving Byzantine-robust FL mechanism, which detects outliers among participants' encrypted updates.

2.8 IMPLEMENTATION

Vanilla FL implementation is given below using PyTorch.

2.8.1 Federated Average

The following code is for the federated averaging (FedAvg).

```
def sub_model(model1, model2):
    params1 = model1.state_dict().copy()
    params2 = model2.state_dict().copy()
    with torch.no_grad():
        for name1 in params1:
            if name1 in params2:
                params1[name1] = params1[name1]
                    - params2[name1]
```

```
 8    model = copy.deepcopy(model1)
 9    model.load_state_dict(params1, strict=False
        )
10    return model
11
12 def add_model(dst_model, src_model):
13    params1 = dst_model.state_dict().copy()
14    params2 = src_model.state_dict().copy()
15    with torch.no_grad():
16        for name1 in params1:
17            if name1 in params2:
18                params1[name1] = params1[name1]
                     + params2[name1]
19    model = copy.deepcopy(dst_model)
20    model.load_state_dict(params1, strict=False
        )
21    return model
22
23 def scale_model(model, scale):
24    params = model.state_dict().copy()
25    scale = torch.tensor(scale)
26    with torch.no_grad():
27        for name in params:
28            params[name] = params[name].type_as
                 (scale) * scale
29    scaled_model = copy.deepcopy(model)
30    scaled_model.load_state_dict(params, strict
        =False)
31    return scaled_model
32
33 def FedAvg(base_model, models):
34    model_list = list(models.values())
35    model = reduce(add_model, model_list)
36    model = scale_model(model, 1.0 /
37    len(models))
38    if base_model is not None:
39        model = sub_model(base_model, model)
40    return model
```

2.8.2 Model Training and Evaluation

The model training and evaluation implementations is as follows.

```
def train_func(_model, data_loader,
    learning_rate, decay, epochs, device):
    model = copy.deepcopy(_model)
    loss = {}
    optimizer = optim.Adam(model.parameters(),
        lr=learning_rate, weight_decay=decay)
    model.train()
    for epoch in range(epochs):
        for batch_idx, (data, target) in
            enumerate(data_loader):
            data, target = data.to(device),
                target.to(device)
            optimizer.zero_grad()
            output = model(data)
            _loss = F.cross_entropy(output,
                target)
            _loss.backward()
            optimizer.step()

        loss["Epoch " + str(epoch + 1)] = _loss
            .item()
    return model, loss

def evaluate(model, test_loader, device):
    model.eval()
    test_output = {
        "test_loss": 0,
        "correct": 0,
        "accuracy": 0
    }

    with torch.no_grad():
        for data, target in test_loader:
            data, target = data.to(device),
                target.to(device)
```

```
29     output = model(data)
30     test_output["test_loss"] += F.
           nll_loss(output, target,
           reduction='sum').item()
31     pred = output.argmax(dim=1, keepdim
           =True)
32     test_output["correct"] += pred.eq(
           target.view_as(pred)).sum().item
           ()
33
34   test_output["test_loss"] /= len(test_loader
         .dataset)
35   test_output["accuracy"] = (test_output["
         correct"] / len(test_loader.dataset)) *
         100
36
37   return test_output
```

2.8.3 Setup

The setup, with loading data to clients, setting up model architecture, parameters, etc. is as follows.

```
1  class FedArgs():
2      def __init__(self):
3          self.name = "client-x"
4          self.num_clients = 100
5          self.epochs = 51
6          self.local_rounds = 1
7          self.client_batch_size = 32
8          self.test_batch_size = 128
9          self.learning_rate = 1e-4
10         self.weight_decay = 1e-5
11         self.cuda = False
12         self.seed = 1
13         self.loop = asyncio.get_event_loop()
14         self.dataset = "mnist"
15         self.labels = [label for label in range
                (10)] # for mnist and f-Mnist
```

```
16        self.model = nn.ModelMNIST() # Any
             torch nn model
17
18 def split_data(train_data, clients):
19     split_arr = [int(len(train_data) / len(
           clients)) for _ in range(len(clients))]
20     rem_data = len(train_data) - sum(split_arr)
21     if rem_data > 0:
22         split_arr[-1] = split_arr[-1] +
               rem_data
23
24     splitted_data = torch.utils.data.
           random_split(train_data, split_arr)
25     clients_data = {client: splitted_data[index
           ] for index, client in enumerate(clients
           )}
26
27     return clients_data
28
29 def load_client_data(clients_data, batch_size,
       **kwargs):
30     train_loaders = {}
31
32     for client, data in clients_data.items():
33         train_loaders[client] = torch.utils.
               data.DataLoader(data, batch_size=
               batch_size, shuffle=True, **kwargs)
34
35     return train_loaders
36
37 fedargs = FedArgs()
38 use_cuda = fedargs.cuda and torch.cuda.
       is_available()
39 device = torch.device("cuda" if use_cuda else "
       CPU")
40 torch.manual_seed(fedargs.seed)
41 kwargs = {"num_workers": 1, "pin_memory": True}
       if use_cuda else {}
42 clients = [str(client + 1) for client in range(
       fedargs.num_clients)]
43
```

```
# Initialize Global and Client models
global_model = copy.deepcopy(fedargs.model)

# Load Data to clients
train_data = datasets.MNIST(root=datadir, train
    =True, transform=transforms.ToTensor(),
    download=True)
test_data = datasets.MNIST(root=datadir, train=
    False, transform=transforms.ToTensor(),
    download=True)

clients_data = split_data(train_data, clients)
client_train_loaders = load_client_data(
    clients_data, fedargs.client_batch_size,
    None, **kwargs)
test_loader = torch.utils.data.DataLoader(
    test_data, batch_size=fedargs.
    test_batch_size, shuffle=True, **kwargs)

client_details = {
        client: {"train_loader":
            client_train_loaders[client],
                "model": copy.deepcopy(
                    global_model),
                "model_update": None}
        for client in clients
    }
```

2.8.4 FL Cycle

The implementation for FL training, aggregation, and evaluation phases is as follows.

```
def background(f):
    def wrapped(*args, **kwargs):
        return asyncio.get_event_loop().
            run_in_executor(None, f, *args, **
            kwargs)

    return wrapped
```

```
@background
def process(client, epoch, model, train_loader,
    device = 'cpu'):
    model_update, model, loss = train_func(
        model, train_loader, fedargs.
        learning_rate, fedargs.weight_decay,
        fedargs.local_rounds, device)

    return model_update

# FL Training and aggregation
for epoch in tqdm(range(fedargs.epochs)):
    if epoch > C:
        # Average
        global_model = FedAvg(
            client_model_updates, global_model)
        global_test_output = evaluate(
            global_model, test_loader, device)

        # Update client models
        for client in clients:
            client_details[client]['model'] =
                copy.deepcopy(global_model)

    # Clients
    tasks = [process(client, epoch,
        client_details[client]['model'],
                    client_details[client]['
                        train_loader'],
                    fedargs, device) for
                        client in clients]
    try:
        updates = fedargs.loop.
            run_until_complete(asyncio.gather(*
            tasks))
    except KeyboardInterrupt as e:
        tasks.cancel()
        fedargs.loop.run_forever()
        tasks.exception()
```

```
34      for client, update in zip(clients, updates)
        :
35          client_details[client]['model_update']
            = update
36      client_model_updates = {client: details["
        model_update"] for client, details in
        client_details.items()}
```

## CHAPTER 3

Poisoning Attacks on FL

$\mathbf{T}$HE DISTRIBUTED NATURE OF federated learning (FL) makes it vulnerable to poisoning attacks. Within the context of FL, an attacker has the potential to control certain malicious clients, as shown in Figure 3.1. These malicious clients can then send random or carefully designed local model updates to the server to achieve the attacker's goal. The malicious clients could be genuine clients who have been compromised by the attacker [18] or fake clients injected by the attacker [12]. In this chapter, we discuss different types of poisoning attacks, such as data and model poisoning attacks. We also detail the adversary goal, knowledge, and capabilities.

3.1 ATTACKER GOAL

The goal of an attacker is to craft local model updates on malicious clients in a way that the resulting global model makes incorrect predictions on a significant number of test inputs (known as *untargeted attacks*) or predicts a predetermined label chosen by the attacker for particular test inputs (known

DOI: 10.1201/9781003688570-3

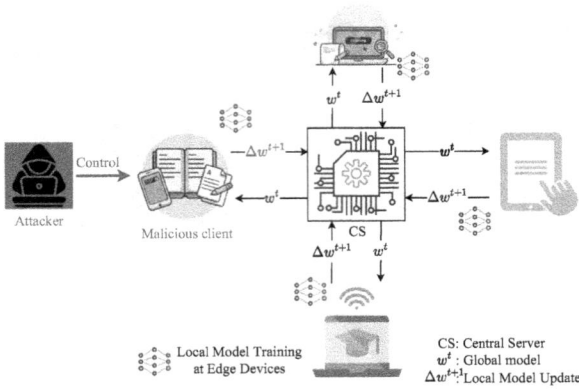

FIGURE 3.1   FL system under poisoning attacks.

as *targeted attacks*). This chapter will present seven state-of-the-art untargeted attacks (Label flipping attack, Gaussian attack, LIE attack, Krum attack, Trim attack, Min-Max attack, and Min-Sum attack) as well as two representative targeted attacks (Scaling attack and Edge attack).

3.2 LABEL FLIPPING ATTACK

Label flipping is a widely studied data poisoning attack in federated learning, where the attacker manipulates only the labels of the training data on malicious clients while keeping the input features unchanged. The goal of this attack is to corrupt the learning process by introducing incorrect labels, either to reduce the overall accuracy of the global model or to cause specific misclassifications.

There are several ways to carry out label flipping on compromised clients. One approach, described by Tolpegin et al. [63], is to flip all instances of a selected *source class* to a chosen *target class*. This targeted mislabeling causes the global model to incorrectly associate the features of the source class with the target class, leading to consistent misclassification errors. Another approach, presented by Fang et al. [18], is to randomly flip each label to a different class. More formally, for each training example with label y, the adversary replaces it with a new label $y' \in \{C \setminus y\}$, where C is the set of all class labels. This random flipping introduces broader label noise into the training data, making it harder to detect using pattern-based or anomaly detection techniques.

3.3 GAUSSIAN ATTACK

The Gaussian attack, introduced by Blanchard et al. [8], is a local model poisoning attack in federated learning where malicious clients deliberately craft and send harmful model updates to the central server. Unlike data poisoning attacks that manipulate training data, this attack manipulates the model updates.

Each compromised client generates a random vector sampled from a Gaussian (normal) distribution with a mean of zero and a high standard deviation, typically set to 200. The generated vectors do not reflect any learning, rather they become intentionally random and uninformative. These malicious updates are then submitted to the server during the aggregation phase, with the intent of disrupting the global model's training process. The large variance in the Gaussian distribution ensures that the submitted updates have high magnitude and variability, which can significantly skew the aggregated model parameters when standard averaging techniques like FedAvg are used.

Because this attack does not require access to any training data or coordination between adversarial clients, it is relatively simple to implement. However, its effectiveness largely depends on the number of malicious clients and the aggregation method used by the server. Poisoning defenses such as robust aggregation rules (e.g., Krum, Trimmed-Mean discussed in Byzantine-robust Defenses) have been proposed to mitigate such high-magnitude outlier attacks.

3.4 LIE ATTACK

The Little is Enough (LIE) attack, proposed by Baruch et al. [6], is a local model poisoning attack that aims to manipulate the global model by introducing small but carefully crafted perturbations. Unlike aggressive attacks that rely on large or random deviations, the LIE attack focuses on subtle manipulations that are statistically similar to benign updates, making the attack stealthy and harder to detect.

The adversary first estimates the distribution of model updates from benign clients. Let μ and σ denote the mean and standard deviation of benign local model updates, respectively. The malicious clients then generate poisoned updates as: Malicious Update $= \mu + \zeta \cdot \sigma$, where ζ is an attack coefficient, adjusted in a way to control the magnitude of the perturbation. By aligning the direction of the attack with the distribution of benign updates, and adjusting the scale using ζ, the adversary ensures that the poisoned updates remain close to the statistical norm of the benign ones. This makes difficult for the server to distinguish through standard poisoning detection mechanisms. Despite their subtlety, these updates can significantly influence the global model over multiple rounds, especially when a sufficient number of clients are compromised. The effectiveness of the LIE attack lies in its balance between stealth and impact: small, coordinated perturbations can gradually bias the learning process without raising suspicion, highlighting the importance of robust aggregation methods and poisoning detection in federated learning systems.

3.5 KRUM ATTACK

The Krum attack [18] is an optimized attack model tailed for Krum [8] aggregation rule. During the Krum attack, the attacker carefully designs the local model updates on malicious clients such that the server mistakenly chooses the malicious local model update as the aggregated model update. Suppose that c out of n clients are malicious. Denote by $w'_1, \cdots, w'_c$ the c malicious local model updates. and by $w_{(c+1)}, \cdots, w_n$ the $n - c$ benign local model updates. The attacker in Krum attack crafts $w'_1, \cdots, w'_c$ via solving the following optimization problem:

$$\max_{\lambda} \lambda \tag{3.1}$$

$$\text{subject to } w'_1 = \text{Krum}(w'_1, \cdots, w'_c, w_{(c+1)}, \cdots, w_n), \tag{3.2}$$

$$w'_1 = w_{Re} - \lambda s, \tag{3.3}$$

$$w'_i = w'_1, \text{ for } i = 2, 3, \cdots, c. \tag{3.4}$$

Equation 3.2 states that if the server uses the Krum aggregation rule to combine all the local model updates sent from clients, the aggregated model update will be w'_1. In Equation 3.3, w_{Re} represents the global model in the previous training round and s denotes the sign of the average of all benign local model updates before the attack. Equation 3.4 shows that the attacker sets the remaining $c - 1$ malicious local model updates as w'_1. From Equations 3.1–3.4, we can observe that the attacker's objective is to maximize the value of λ in order to increase the testing error rate of the final learned global model.

In an FL setup with 100 participants, 20 of them are malicious. We train a convolutional neural network (CNN) on the MNIST [40] dataset, with the structure of CNN detailed in Table 3.1. We train the CNN model for 5000 global training

TABLE 3.1   The CNN Architecture for MNIST Dataset

Layer	Size
Input	$28 \times 28 \times 1$
Convolution − ReLU	$3 \times 3 \times 30$
Max Pooling	2×2
Convolution − ReLU	$3 \times 3 \times 50$
Max Pooling	2×2
Fully Connected + ReLU	100
Softmax	10

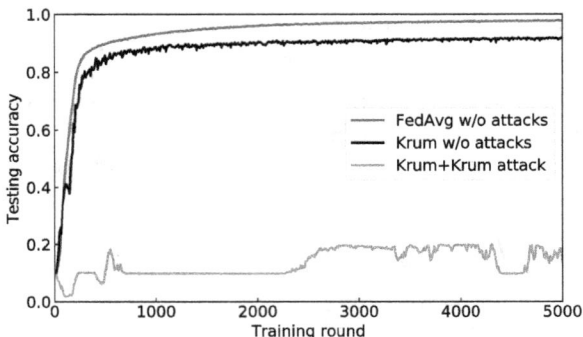

FIGURE 3.2   Testing accuracy of Krum aggregation rule under Krum attack on MNIST dataset.

rounds. Each client uses a learning rate of $1/3200$ and a batch size 32. In FL, the training data are not independent and identically distributed (non-IID) among participants. To emulate the MNIST dataset's non-IID nature, we follow the method in [18]. Specifically, given a dataset with C classes, we categorize clients into C groups, with MNIST having $C = 10$ groups. If a training sample is labeled as y, it is allocated to clients in group y and to other groups with a probability of $\frac{1-p}{C-1}$. Here, p dictates the non-IID level. For the clients in the same group, the training examples are uniformly distributed. A higher p value means a higher level of non-IID, $p = \frac{1}{C}$ for complete IID distribution. In our study, we set $p = 0.5$ for the MNIST dataset. Figure 3.2 shows the testing accuracy of the global model on the MNIST dataset. In Figure 3.2, "FedAvg w/o attacks" and "Krum w/o attacks" mean all clients are benign, and the server leverages the FedAvg and Krum aggregation rules to combine the local model updates, respectively. "Krum+Krum attack" refers to the server combining the local model updates it receives using the Krum aggregation technique. Meanwhile, the attacker crafts malicious model updates using the Krum attack. We observe that the Krum attack can considerably reduce the test accuracy of the global model when targeting the Krum aggregation method.

3.6 TRIM ATTACK

The Trim attack [18] is a specific attack model designed to target the Trimmed-mean [75] and Median [75] aggregation rules. The idea behind the Trim attack is that the attacker manipulates the model updates on malicious clients so that the aggregated model after the attack deviates (both direction and magnitude) substantially from the before-attack one. Specifically, the attacker crafts the malicious model updates by solving the optimization problem defined as follows:

$$\max_{w'_1, \cdots, u'_c} s^\top (w - w'), \tag{3.5}$$

$$\text{subject to } w = \mathcal{A}(w_1, \cdots, w_c, w_{c+1}, \cdots, w_n), \tag{3.6}$$

$$w' = \mathcal{A}(w'_1, \cdots, w'_c, w_{c+1}, \cdots, w_n), \tag{3.7}$$

where $w'_1, \cdots, w'_c$ are c malicious model updates; $w_1, \cdots, w_c$, $w_{c+1}, \cdots, w_n$ are n before-attack local model updates; w is the aggregated model update before attack; w' is the aggregated model update after attack; s represents the sign of the average of all benign local model updates before attack; $s^\top$ denotes the transpose of vector s; $\mathcal{A}$ is the aggregation rule used by the server, such as Trimmed-mean [75] and Median [75].

3.7 SHEJWALKAR ATTACK

In [60], the authors proposed a general poisoning attack framework. This framework seeks to maximize the distance between the average local model update prior to the attack and the aggregated model update after the attack. Let $\text{Avg}(w_1, \cdots, w_n)$ represent the average local model before the attack and w' denote the after-attack aggregated model update, then one has the following optimization problem:

$$\arg\max_{\lambda,\Delta} \quad \|\text{Avg}(w_1,\cdots,w_n) - w'\|_2, \qquad (3.8)$$

$$\text{subject to } w' = \mathcal{A}(w'_1,\cdots,w'_c,w_{c+1},\cdots,w_n) \qquad (3.9)$$

$$w'_1 = \text{Avg}(w_1,\cdots,w_n) + \lambda\Delta, \qquad (3.10)$$

$$w'_i = w'_1, \text{ for } i = 2,3,\cdots,c, \qquad (3.11)$$

where λ is a scaling coefficient, Δ is a perturbation vector, $\mathcal{A}$ is any aggregation rule used by the server. From Equation 3.10, we observe that in the Shejwalkar attack, each malicious local model update can be considered a perturbed version of the before-attack average model update. Solving the aforementioned optimization problem is challenging because it requires simultaneous optimization of parameters λ and Δ. To overcome this, the authors in [60] fix the perturbation vector Δ and optimize the scaling coefficient λ. Consequently, this leads to the following optimization problem:

$$\arg\max_{\lambda} \quad \|\text{Avg}(w_1,\cdots,w_n) - w'\|_2, \qquad (3.12)$$

$$\text{subject to } w' = \mathcal{A}(w'_1,\cdots,w'_c,w_{c+1},\cdots,w_n) \qquad (3.13)$$

$$w'_1 = \text{Avg}(w_1,\cdots,w_n) + \lambda\Delta, \qquad (3.14)$$

$$w'_i = w'_1, \text{ for } i = 2,3,\cdots,c. \qquad (3.15)$$

where Δ is a fixed vector, which could be an inverse unit vector ($\Delta = -\frac{\text{Avg}(w_1,\cdots,w_n)}{\|\text{Avg}(w_1,\cdots,w_n)\|_2}$) or an inverse sign vector ($\Delta = -\text{sign}(\text{Avg}(w_1,\cdots,w_n))$).

3.7.1 Min-Max Attack

In Min-Max attack [60], the attacker does not know the aggregation rule used by the server and ensures that the malicious local model updates are not far from the cluster of benign local model updates. Let $[n]$ denote the set $\{1,\cdots,n\}$. The Min-Max attack is formulated as the following optimization problem:

$$\arg\max_{\lambda} \quad \max_{i\in[n]} \|w_1' - w_i\|_2 \le \max_{i,j\in[n]} \|w_i - w_j\|_2,$$
(3.16)

$$\text{subject to } w_1' = \text{Avg}(w_1, \cdots, w_n) + \lambda\Delta, \tag{3.17}$$

$$w_i' = w_1', \text{ for } i = 2, 3, \cdots, c. \tag{3.18}$$

We observe from Equation 3.16 that the maximum distance between a malicious model update w_1' and any benign model update is not larger than the maximum distance between any two benign model updates. In Equation 3.17, Avg() is the average aggregation rule and Δ is a perturbation vector. It can be computed as the negative sign of the average of all benign local model updates before the attack, i.e., $\Delta = -\text{sign}(\text{Avg}(w_1, \cdots, w_n))$. Like in the Krum attack [18], the attacker keeps all the malicious model updates identical in the Min-Max attack.

3.7.2 Min-Sum Attack

Min-Sum [60] is another aggregation rule agnostic attack model. In the Min-Sum attack, the attacker guarantees that the sum of squared distances between a malicious model update w_1' and any benign model update is not larger than the sum of squared distances between any two benign model updates. Specifically, the following optimization problem is formulated to craft the malicious model updates.

$$\arg\max_{\lambda} \quad \sum_{i\in[n]} \|w_1' - w_i\|_2^2 \le \max_{i\in[n]} \sum_{j\in[n]} \|w_i - w_j\|_2^2$$
(3.19)

$$\text{subject to } w_1' = \text{Avg}(w_1, \cdots, w_n) + \lambda\Delta, \tag{3.20}$$

$$w_i' = w_1', \text{ for } i = 2, 3, \cdots, c. \tag{3.21}$$

3.8 SINE ATTACK

In this work [37], the authors propose a novel local model poisoning attack, called SINE (similarity is not enough) against

FL aggregation schemes that rely on similarity-based defenses. The intuition is to exploit the fact that similarity metrics alone are not sufficient to distinguish malicious updates from benign ones when the malicious updates are explicitly optimized to appear similar. A malicious client replaces its standard local update Δw_{benign} with a carefully crafted adversarial update $\Delta w_{\text{malicious}}$ that is optimized to achieve two objectives: (i) maximize its malicious impact on the global model and (ii) remain similar to benign updates to avoid detection by robust aggregation rules.

In this attack, the authors extended the threat models from [18] and introduced different attack knowledge and capabilities. The attacker can either have knowledge of the aggregation rule or not, which can be mentioned as: AK – Aggregation rule known or AN – Aggregation rule not known. Further, they highlighted that their attack was initially tailored to FLTrust (a poisoning defense discussed later in Byzantine-robust Defenses), so they considered another knowledge category called AK-BSU (Aggregation Rule Known with Base Server Update). In terms of attacker capabilities, they introduced individual capabilities in addition to full and partial capabilities. In individual capability, given m of n participants are malicious in nature, still they work independently without knowing/communicating about each other. This is important because, if such an attack is successful, it is very dangerous to the system. On the contrary, it is assumed that attackers know about all other participants in the system, in the full attack capabilities. This attack is only framed to test the defense mechanism in the worst possible scenario. Partial attack capability is the most natural attack capabilities, where all the attackers know about each other and are able to communicate and frame the attack together.

3.8.1 Attack Procedure

In each communication round t, a trusted server disseminates the current global model w^t to all participants. All participants, including both honest and compromised clients, first perform benign local model training. Among compromised clients, a coordinating adversary, called as CL, collects the benign updates from the compromised clients and computes their average, which we refer to as the baseline vector B.

In addition, CL performs local training using the same global model w^t and obtains its own benign update, denoted as $C = \nabla_{CL}^t$. The attacker's goal is to derive a malicious model update M that closely resembles C (to evade detection) while being significantly dissimilar from B (to degrade model performance or influence aggregation). The intuition as discussed before (similar to LIE attack) is to have more supporters in the system.

Moreover, many such vectors M may exist in a high-dimensional space, the attacker selects a deterministic one using a specific optimization strategy. The process begins by initializing $M \leftarrow B$. Two hyperparameters are used: γ_c, a factor used to scale cosine similarity computations, and γ_n, which defines the permissible range of deviation in the norm of M relative to C. The attacker identifies the coordinates where B and C differ the most and prioritizes these for modification. Iteratively, for each such coordinate k, the attacker attempts to adjust the value in M to make it more aligned with C in the direction but less similar to B. This is achieved by solving a constraint where the cosine similarity between the modified M and C equals the cosine similarity between the current M and C, scaled by γ_c. The solution generated two candidates for the new value at coordinate k; it is only adopted if it decreases the similarity to B without violating the similarity condition with C. This iterative process continues across coordinates, each time verifying two criteria: (1) the updated vector maintains a cosine similarity to C close to the desired threshold and (2) the vector norm lies within a range defined by $\left[\frac{1}{\gamma_n} \cdot \|C\|, \gamma_n \cdot \|C\|\right]$. If these checks are passed, the modified vector becomes the new candidate for M; otherwise, the modification is discarded.

Once the malicious update M has been finalized, each adversarial client prepares its own submission for aggregation. Depending on the attacker's capability, this submission process differs:

- In the *individual capability* setting, each attacker independently crafts a malicious update using its own benign model as a baseline.

- In *partial or full capabilities*, the attackers use the shared M, adding a small random perturbation ϵ_i to avoid detection by Sybil-resilient defenses.

3.9 SCALING ATTACK

The Scaling attack, introduced by Bagdasaryan et al. [5], is a targeted model poisoning attack in federated learning that enables adversaries to inject backdoors into the global model. The attack proceeds in multiple stages. Initially, the adversary duplicates the local training dataset available to each compromised (malicious) client. Into these duplicated examples, specific input patterns (referred to as *triggers*) are embedded. The labels corresponding to these trigger-embedded examples are then overwritten with a pre-defined target label selected by the attacker, thereby constructing a backdoor training set.

Subsequently, each malicious client performs local training using a combination of its original benign dataset and the backdoor augmented dataset. After completing local training, instead of directly submitting the resulting model update to the central server, each adversarial client amplifies its update by multiplying it with a carefully chosen *scaling factor*. This scaling factor is designed to disproportionately influence the global aggregation, thereby increasing the likelihood that the global model gets impacted by the backdoor behavior.

As a result, once the federated learning process converges, the global model exhibits the intended backdoor functionality: inputs that include the trigger pattern are misclassified into the target class with high probability, while its performance on clean, non-triggered inputs remains largely unaffected. This deceptive property makes the attack stealthy and difficult to detect.

It is important to note that when the scaling factor is set to one (i.e., no amplification is applied), the attack degenerates into a conventional data poisoning attack. In such cases, the malicious behavior arises solely from the poisoned data distribution rather than from an over-weighted influence during model aggregation.

3.10 EDGE ATTACK

The Edge attack, proposed by Wang et al. [64], is another targeted model poisoning strategy within FL settings. This attack focuses on exploiting the vulnerability of models by utilizing/crafting training samples located near the decision boundaries, referred to as *edge examples*. The adversary augments the local training data of each compromised client with these edge examples, which are specifically chosen or crafted to lie close to the classification boundaries between the target class and other classes. These examples are then labeled with an attacker-specified target class to construct a backdoor dataset.

Each malicious client subsequently performs local training using both of its benign dataset and the augmented (label-poisoned) dataset. Similar to the Scaling attack, the resulting local model update is then amplified by a *scaling factor* before being transmitted to the server. The objective of this amplification is to increase the relative influence of the poisoned updates in the global aggregation process, thereby embedding the backdoor functionality into the global model more effectively.

A key insight provided by the authors in [64] is the connection between a model's susceptibility to adversarial perturbations at inference time and its vulnerability to backdoor attacks during training. Specifically, if a model is easily fooled by small, imperceptible perturbations during inference, it is also more likely to include malicious behaviors, such as those introduced via backdoor or edge-triggered examples during training. This insight underscores the fragility of the global model and the difficulty in detecting well-designed backdoors, especially when the poisoned updates mimic benign behavior in terms of loss convergence and gradient similarity.

Overall, the Edge attack poses a significant threat to federated learning, as it stealthily manipulates the model's decision boundaries while avoiding detection by conventional server-side defenses.

3.11 VULNERABILITIES IN COSINE SIMILARITY-BASED DEFENSES

Layer replacement attack (LRA) and cosine similarity attack [35] are local model poisoning attacks framed against cosine similarity-based defenses. The potential vulnerabilities in cosine similarity-based defenses are as follows:

1. Only multidimensional sparse models can benefit from cosine similarity. As a result, it is only applicable to the client's local model updates. In contrast, it cannot be applied to the client's (complete) models (since they are dense) or layer-by-layer (because there are fewer dimensions).

2. Given vectors $\vec{A}$ and $\vec{B}$, it is possible to find multiple vectors $(\vec{C})$ around the conic axis of $\vec{A}$, such that the cosine similarity of $\vec{A}$ and $\vec{C}$ is equal to the cosine similarity of $\vec{A}$ and $\vec{B}$.

LRA harnesses the first vulnerability to frame a local model poisoning attack. In this attack, the malicious client can inject malicious layers between its local model updates that will affect the model's performance without deviating significantly from the direction. Changing a few significant weights in a layer does not impact the cosine similarity much but it impacts the model's accuracy significantly. These weights can be found using different methods, such as model importance (neuron Shapley [24]). Further enhancement in attack can be achieved through backdooring layers generated from maliciously trained models, such as backdoored or label-flipped models.

CSA harnesses the second vulnerability to frame a local model poisoning attack. An adversary can create an identical-looking malicious model update that is fundamentally different, thereby causing poisoning and impacting model performance. Thus, a malicious client can find a local model update that appears to be benign but is malicious in behavior. The malicious client can assume the previous global model update as $\vec{A}$, trains a benign model update to get $\vec{B}$, and finds a malicious vector $\vec{C}$ around the conic axis of $\vec{A}$, such that the cosine similarity of $\vec{A}$ and $\vec{C}$ is equal to the cosine similarity of $\vec{A}$ and $\vec{B}$.

Using the same vulnerability, authors in [36] proposed to generate poisoned (adversarial) samples by projecting an input sample to an enormous hyperdimensional (HD) space and the perturbation of the HD sample in proximity to the target (attack) HD class model. Data is represented and manipulated using high-dimensional vectors in HD computing (HDC) [34].

Figure 3.3 demonstrates the methodology to generate targeted adversarial samples, which can be used further for data poisoning. The adversary wants the samples from the source class (S) to get misclassified as the target class (T). Then, the adversary generates the targeted adversarial (poisoned)

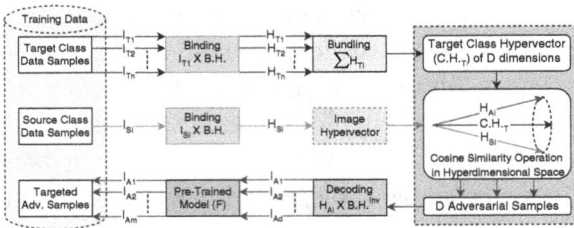

FIGURE 3.3   Adversarial sample generation. D is hyperdimenisonal space, and m out of D samples are misclassified as target class. IT = Image of Target Class; B.H. = Base Hypervector; HT = Hypervector of Target Class; IS = Image of Source Class; HS = Hypervector of Source Class; IA = Adversarial Images.

samples in three steps: (1) generate target class hypervector by bundling after binding multiple data samples from the target class; (2) generate source class hypervector by binding a data sample from the source class; (3) using both the hypervectors, a new (malicious) hypervector can be created harnessing the second potential vulnerability in cosine similarity. Finally, the adversary can train a poisoned model using these generated samples.

Table 3.2 compares the poisoning attacks in FL. The data poisoning attacks such as label flipping, scaling, and edge attacks are deterministic in nature and easy to frame. They are also aggregation agnostic and incur less computational cost. Meanwhile, local model poisoning attacks such as LIE, Fang (Krum and Trim), Shejwalkar attacks solve an optimization problem to find the malicious model updates, while *Sine* aims to design a deterministic aggregation agnostic attack. This ensures the effectiveness in both the attack impact and computational cost.

TABLE 3.2 Comparison between Model Poisoning Attacks

Attack	Det.	non-IID	Agg. Agnostic	Adversary Capabilities	Computation
Label Flipping	✓	✓	✓	Partial	Low
Scaling	✓	✓	✓	Partial	Low
Edge	✓	✓	✓	Partial	Low
Gaussian	✓	✓	✓	Full	Low
LIE	✗	✗	✗	Full	High
Fang	✗	✓	✗	Full and Partial	High
Shejwalkar	✗	✓	✓	Full and Partial	High
Sine	✓	✓	✓	Full, Partial and Individual	Medium

Note: Det. = Deterministic, Agg. = Aggregation rule

3.12 IMPLEMENTATION

3.12.1 Helper Libraries

We implemented a helper library, sim.py, which performs the following calculations:

1. Norm of an array: `norm(arr)`

2. Norm of a model: `grad_norm(model)`

3. Min-max normalization of an array: `min_max_norm(arr)`

4. Euclidean distance between two arrays: `eucliden_dist(arr1, arr2)`

5. Euclidean distance between two model gradients: `grad_eucliden_dist(model1, model2)`

6. Cosine similarity between two arrays: `cosine_similarity(arr1, arr2)`

7. Cosine similarity between two model gradients: `grad_cosine_similarity(model1, model2)`

8. Dot product between two arrays: `dot(arr1, arr2)`

9. Cosine similar vector: `cosine_coord_vector_adapter(A, B, coordinate_to_change, dot_AB, norm_B, cos_sim_BC, C, norm_C, norm_B, **kwargs)`

10. One-dimensional representation of model: `def get_mx_net_arr(model):` or `get_net_arr(model)`

11. Model from one-dimensional representation: `get_arr_net(_model, arr, slist)`

These functions can be referred from below.

```
1   import copy, cmath, torch
2   import numpy as nd
3   from mxnet import nd as mnd
4
5   def norm(arr):
6       return mnd.norm(mnd.array(arr)).asnumpy()
            [0]
7
8   def grad_norm(model):
9       arr, _ = get_net_arr(model)
10      return norm(arr)
11
12  def min_max_norm(arr):
13      if (max(arr) - min(arr)) != 0:
14          return (arr - min(arr)) / (max(arr) -
                min(arr))
15      else:
16          return arr
17
18  def eucliden_dist(arr1, arr2):
19      return nd.linalg.norm(arr1-arr2)
20
21  def grad_eucliden_dist(model1, model2):
22      arr1, _ = get_net_arr(model1)
23      arr2, _ = get_net_arr(model2)
24      return eucliden_dist(arr1, arr2)
25
```

```
def cosine_similarity(arr1, arr2):
    cs = mnd.dot(mnd.array(arr1), mnd.array(
        arr2)) / (mnd.norm(mnd.array(arr1)) + 1e
        -9) / (mnd.norm(mnd.array(arr2)) + 1e-9)
    return cs.asnumpy()[0]


def grad_cosine_similarity(model1, model2):
    arr1, _ = get_net_arr(model1)
    arr2, _ = get_net_arr(model2)
    return cosine_similarity(arr1, arr2)


def dot(arr1, arr2):
    cs = mnd.dot(mnd.array(arr1), mnd.array
        (arr2))
    return cs.asnumpy()[0]


def cosine_coord_vector_adapter(b, m, coord,
    dot_mb, norm_m, sim_mg, c, norm_c, norm_b,
    **kwargs):
    scale_norm = kwargs["scale_norm"] if "
        scale_norm" in kwargs else 10

    prev_m_coord = m[coord]
    m[coord] = cosine_coord_vector(b, m, coord,
        dot_mb, norm_m)

    _dot_mg = (sim_mg * norm_m * norm_c) - (c[
        coord] * (prev_m_coord - m[coord]))
    _norm_m = cmath.sqrt(norm_m**2 -
        prev_m_coord**2 + m[coord]**2)
    _sim_mg = (_dot_mg / (_norm_m * norm_c)).
        real


    updated = True
    if _sim_mg < sim_mg and _norm_m < (norm_b *
        scale_norm) and _norm_m > (norm_b * (1
        / scale_norm)):
```

```
          sim_mg = _sim_mg
          norm_m = _norm_m
          dot_mb = dot_mb - b[coord] *
          (prev_m_coord - m[coord])
      else:
          updated = False
          m[coord] = prev_m_coord

      return m, dot_mb, norm_m, sim_mg, updated


def cosine_coord_vector(b, m, coord, dot_mb=
    None, norm_m = None):
      if dot_mb is None:
          dot_mb = dot(b, m)
      if norm_m is None:
          norm_m = norm(m)

      lhs = ((dot_mb / norm_m) ** 2)


      coeff_b_coord = b[coord]
      coeff_m_coord = m[coord]


      _dot_mb = dot_mb - (coeff_m_coord *
          coeff_b_coord)
      _norm_m = norm_m**2 - (coeff_m_coord**2)


      deg_2 = lhs - (coeff_b_coord**2)
      deg_1 = -2 * _dot_mb * coeff_b_coord
      deg_0 = lhs * _norm_m - (_dot_mb**2)


      d = (deg_1**2) - (4*deg_2*deg_0)
      d_sqrt = cmath.sqrt(d)
      _denom = 2*deg_2
      sol1 = ((-deg_1-d_sqrt)/(_denom)).real
      sol2 = ((-deg_1+d_sqrt)/(_denom)).real
```

```
 95        sol = sol1
 96        if abs(scl2 - coeff_m_coord) > abs(sol1 -
               coeff_m_coord):
 97            sol = sol2
 98
 99        return scl
100
101
102   def get_mx_net_arr(model):
103        param_list = [param.data.numpy() for param
               in model.parameters()]
104        _param_list = nd.array(param_list).squeeze
               ()
105
106        arr = nd.array([[]])
107        for index, item in enumerate(_param_list):
108            item = item.reshape((-1, 1))
109            if index == 0:
110                arr = item
111            else:
112                arr = nd.concatenate((arr, item),
                       axis=0)
113
114        arr = nd.array(arr).squeeze()
115        arr = mnd.array(arr)
116        return arr
117
118
119   def get_net_arr(model):
120        param_list = [param.data.numpy() for param
               in model.parameters()]
121
122        arr = nd.array([[]])
123        slist = []
124        for index, item in enumerate(param_list):
125            slist.append(item.shape)
126            item = item.reshape((-1, 1))
127            if index == 0:
128                arr = item
129            else:
```

```
130            arr = nd.concatenate((arr, item),
                  axis=0)
131
132        arr = nd.array(arr).squeeze()
133
134        return arr, list
135
136    def get_arr_net(_model, arr, slist):
137        arr = torch.from_numpy(arr).unsqueeze(1)
138        arr = arr.numpy()
139
140        _param_list = []
141        start_index = 0
142        for shape in slist:
143            end_index = start_index + nd.prod(list(
                  shape))
144            item = arr[start_index:end_index]
145            start_index = end_index
146            item = item.reshape(shape)
147            _param_list.append(item)
148
149        params = _model.state_dict().copy()
150        with torch.no_grad():
151            _index = 0
152            for name in params:
153                if "weight" in name or "bias" in
                      name:
154                    params[name] = torch.from_numpy
                          (_param_list[_index])
155                    _index = _index + 1
156
157        model = copy.deepcopy(_model)
158        model.load_state_dict(params, strict=False)
159
160        return model
```

3.12.2 Label Flipping Attack

The above-discussed label-flipping attack can be implemented as follows.

```
def label_flip_next(data, flip_labels,
    poison_percent = 0.5):    data = list(data)

    poison_count = poison_percent * len(data)
    if poison_percent == -1:
        poison_count = len(data)

    label_poisoned = 0
    for index, _ in enumerate(data):
        data[index] = list(data[index])
        if data[index][1] in flip_labels.keys()
            :
            data[index][1] = flip_labels[data[
                index][1]]
            label_poisoned += 1
        data[index] = tuple(data[index])
        if label_poisoned >= poison_count:
            break

    return tuple(data)
```

3.12.3 Trim Attack

The above-discussed Trim attack [18] can be implemented as follows.

```
import sim
from mxnet import nd as mnd

def fang_trmean(models, f, kn = Knowledge.
    PartialKnowledge):
    model_list = list(models.values())
    model_keys = list(models.keys())
```

```
v = []
if kn is Knowledge.PartialKnowledge:
    model_list = model_list[:f]

for model in model_list:
    model_arr = sim.get_mx_net_arr(model)
    v.append(model_arr.reshape(-1, 1))

# local model poisoning attack against
    Trimmed-mean
vi_shape = v[0].shape
v_tran = mnd.concat(*v, dim=1)
maximum_dim = mnd.max(v_tran, axis=1).
    reshape(vi_shape)
minimum_dim = mnd.min(v_tran, axis=1).
    reshape(vi_shape)
direction = mnd.sign(mnd.sum(mnd.concat(*v,
    dim=1), axis=-1, keepdims=True))
directed_dim = (direction > 0) *
    minimum_dim + (direction < 0) *
    maximum_dim
# let the malicious clients (first f
    clients) perform the attack
for i in range(f):
    random_12 = 1. + mnd.random.uniform
    (shape=vi_shape)
    v[i] = directed_dim * ((direction *
        directed_dim > 0) / random_12 +
    (direction * directed_dim < 0) *
        random_12)

dummy_model = model_list[0]
_, d_shape = sim.get_net_arr(dummy_model)

for index in range(f):
    models[model_keys[index]] = sim.
        get_arr_net(dummy_model, v[index].
        asnumpy(), d_shape)

return models
```

3.12.4 LIE Attack

The above-discussed LIE attack [6] can be implemented as follows.

```
import sim
import torch
import numpy as np

def lie_attack(models, n_attackers, kn =
    Knowledge.PartialKnowledge):
    model_list = list(models.values())
    model_keys = list(models.keys())

    dummy_model = model_list[0]
    _, d_shape = sim.get_net_arr(dummy_model)

    v = []
    if kn is Knowledge.PartialKnowledge:
        model_list = model_list[:n_attackers]

    for model in model_list:
        model_arr, _ = sim.get_net_arr(model)
        v.append(model_arr)

    avg = np.array(v).mean(0)
    std = torch.std(torch.tensor(v), 0)

    z_values={3:0.69847, 5:0.7054, 8:0.71904,
        10:0.72575, 12:0.73891}

    mal_update = avg + z_values[n_attackers] *
        std.numpy()

    for index in range(n_attackers):
        models[model_keys[index]] = sim.
            get_arr_net(dummy_model, mal_update,
            d_shape)

    return models
```

3.12.5 Min-max Attack

The above-discussed min-max attack [60] can be implemented as follows.

```
import sim
import torch
import numpy as np

def min_max(models, n_attackers, kn = Knowledge
    .PN, dev_type='unit_vec'):
    model_list = list(models.values())
    model_keys = list(models.keys())

    dummy_model = model_list[0]
    _, d_shape = sim.get_net_arr(dummy_model)

    v = []
    if kn is Knowledge.PN:
        model_list = model_list[:n_attackers]

    for model in model_list:
        model_arr, _ = sim.get_net_arr(model)
        v.append(model_arr)
    model_re = np.array(v).mean(0)

    if dev_type == 'sign':
        deviation = np.sign(model_re)
    elif dev_type == 'unit_vec':
        # unit vector, dir opp to good dir
        deviation = model_re / sim.norm
            (model_re)
    elif dev_type == 'std':
        deviation = torch.std(v, 0)

    lamda = torch.Tensor([50.0]).float()
    threshold_diff = 1e-5
    lamda_fail = lamda
    lamda_succ = 0

    distances = []
    for _v in v:
```

```
distance = torch.norm((torch.tensor(v)
    - torch.tensor(_v)), dim=1) ** 2
distances = distance[None, :] if not
    len(distances) else torch.cat
    ((distances, distance[None, :]), 0)

max_distance = torch.max(distances)
del distances

while torch.abs(lamda_succ - lamda) >
    threshold_diff:
    mal_update = (model_re - (lamda *
        deviation).numpy())
    distance = torch.norm((torch.tensor(v)
        - torch.tensor(mal_update)), dim=1)
        ** 2
    max_d = torch.max(distance)

    if max_d <= max_distance:
        lamda_succ = lamda
        lamda = lamda + lamda_fail / 2
    else:
        lamda = lamda - lamda_fail / 2

    lamda_fail = lamda_fail / 2

mal_update = (model_re - (lamda *
deviation).numpy())

for index in range(n_attackers):
    models[model_keys[index]] = sim.
        get_arr_net(dummy_model, mal_update,
        d_shape)

return models
```

3.12.6 Min-sum Attack

The above-discussed min-sum attack [60] can be implemented as follows.

```python
import sim
import torch
import numpy as np

def min_sum(models, n_attackers, kn = Knowledge
    .PN, dev_type='unit_vec'):
    model_list = list(models.values())
    model_keys = list(models.keys())

    dummy_model = model_list[0]
    _, d_shape = sim.get_net_arr(dummy_model)

    v = []
    if kn is Knowledge.PN:
        model_list = model_list[:n_attackers]

    for model in model_list:
        model_arr, _ = sim.get_net_arr(model)
        v.append(model_arr)
    model_re = np.array(v).mean(0)

    if dev_type == 'sign':
        deviation = np.sign(model_re)
    elif dev_type == 'unit_vec':
        # unit vector, dir opp to good dir
        deviation = model_re / sim.norm(
            model_re)
    elif dev_type == 'std':
        deviation = torch.std(v, 0)

    lamda = torch.Tensor([50.0]).float()
    threshold_diff = 1e-5
    lamda_fail = lamda
    lamda_succ = 0

    distances = []
    for _v in v:
```

```
        distance = torch.norm((torch.tensor(v)
            - torch.tensor(_v)), dim=1) ** 2
        distances = distance[None, :] if not
            len(distances) else torch.cat((
            distances, distance[None, :]), 0)

    scores = torch.sum(distances, dim=1)
    min_score = torch.min(scores)
    del distances

    while torch.abs(lamda_succ - lamda) >
        threshold_diff:
        mal_update = (model_re - (lamda *
            deviation).numpy())
        distance = torch.norm((torch.tensor(v)
            - torch.tensor(mal_update)), dim=1)
            ** 2
        score = torch.sum(distance)

        if score <= min_score:
            lamda_succ = lamda
            lamda = lamda + lamda_fail / 2
        else:
            lamda = lamda - lamda_fail / 2

        lamda_fail = lamda_fail / 2

    mal_update = (model_re - (lamda *
    deviation).numpy())

    for index in range(n_attackers):
        models[model_keys[index]] = sim.
            get_arr_net(dummy_model, mal_update,
            d_shape)

    return models
```

3.12.7 SINE Poisoning Attack

The above-discussed SINE (similarity is not enough) attack [36] can be implemented as follows.

```
from functools import partial
from multiprocessing import Pool, Process
import sim
import numpy as np

def model_poison_cosine_coord(b_arr, cos_args,
    c_arr):
    poison_percent = cos_args["poison_percent"]
        if "poison_percent" in cos_args else 1
    scale_dot = cos_args["scale_dot"] if "
        scale_dot" in cos_args else 1

    print("*before",sim.cosine_similarity(c_arr
        , b_arr))

    npd = c_arr - b_arr
    p_arr = copy.deepcopy(c_arr)

    dot_mb = scale_dot * sim.dot(p_arr, b_arr)
    norm_b = sim.norm(b_arr)
    norm_c = sim.norm(c_arr)
    norm_m = norm_c
    sim_mg = 1

    kwargs = {"scale_norm": cos_args
        ["scale_norm"]} if "scale_norm"
        in cos_args else {}

    for index in heapq.nlargest(int(len(npd) *
        poison_percent), range(len(npd)), npd.
        take):
        p_arr, dot_mb, norm_m, sim_mg, updated
            = sim.cosine_coord_vector_adapter(
            b_arr, p_arr, index, dot_mb, norm_m,
            sim_mg, c_arr, norm_c, norm_b, **
            kwargs)
```

```
28      params_changed = len(npd) - np.sum(p_arr ==
            c_arr)

30      print("*after1', sim.cosine_similarity
31      (p_arr, b_arr))
32      print("*after2', sim.cosine_similarity
33      (p_arr, c_arr))

35      return p_arr, params_changed

37  def sine_attack(base_model_update, cosine_args,
        epoch, models, n_attackers, kn = Knowledge.
        IN):
38      model_list = list(models.values())
39      mal_updates = []
40      params_changed = 0

42      b_arr, b_list = sim.get_net_arr
43      (base_model_update)

45      if epoch % cosine_args["scale_epoch"] == 0:
46          cosine_args["scale_dot"] = cosine_args
                ["scale_dot_factor"] + cosine_args["
                scale_dot"]
47          cosine_args["scale_norm"] = cosine_args
                ["scale_norm_factor"] * cosine_args
                ["scale_norm"]

49      if kn is Knowledge.IN:
50          with Pool(n_attackers) as p:
51              func = partial
52              (model_poison_cosine_coord, b_arr,
                    cosine_args)
53              p_models = p.map(func, [sim.
                    get_net_arr(model_list
54              [attacker])[0] for attacker in
                    range
55              (n_attackers)])
56              p.close()
57              p.join()
```

```
mal_updates = [sim.get_arr_net
(base_model_update, p_arr, b_list) for
    p_arr, _ in p_models]
params_changed = p_models[0][1]
else:
    if kn is Knowledge.PN:
        model_list = model_list[:
            n_attackers]
    elif kn is Knowledge.FN:
        model_list = model_list
        [n_attackers:]

    model_re = np.array([sim.get_net_arr(
        model)[0] for model in model_list]).
        mean(0)
    p_model_arr, params_changed =
        model_poison_cosine_coord(b_arr,
        cosine_args, model_re)
    p_model = sim.get_arr_net
    (base_model_update, p_model_arr, b_list
        )

    mal_updates = [p_model for attacker in
        range(n_attackers)]

return mal_updates, params_changed
```

3.12.8 HDC-based Data Poisoning Attack

The above-discussed data poisoning attack [36] using HDC can be implemented as follows.

```
import sim
import torch
import numpy as np

class HDC(torch.nn.Module):
    def __init__(self, img_len, hvd,
        num_classes, device = 'cpu'):
        super(HDC, self).__init__()
```

```
  8        self.cos = torch.nn.CosineSimilarity(
               dim=-1, eps=1e-8)
  9        self.num_classes = num_classes
 10        self.hvd=hvd
 11        self.b_proj = np.random.randint(2, size
               =(img_len, hvd))
 12        self.b_proj[np.isclose(self.b_proj, 0)]
               = -1
 13        self.proj = torch.rand((img_len, hvd),
               device=device)
 14        self.proj_inv = self.get_proj_inv()
 15        self.train_vectors = torch.zeros
 16        ((num_classes, hvd), device=device)
 17
 18    def get_proj_inv(self):
 19        proj_trans = torch.transpose(self.proj,
               0, 1)
 20        proj_mul_trans = self.proj @ proj_trans
 21        proj_mul_trans_inv = torch.inverse(
               proj_mul_trans)
 22        proj_inv = proj_trans @
               proj_mul_trans_inv
 23        return proj_inv
 24
 25    def train(self, train_loader, device):
 26        x_train, y_train = next(iter(
               train_loader))
 27        x_train, y_train = x_train.to(device),
               y_train.to(device)
 28
 29        hdc_train = x_train.reshape(x_train.
               shape[0], -1) @ self.proj
 30
 31        for i in range(x_train.shape[0]):
 32            self.train_vectors[y_train[i]] +=
                   hdc_train[i]
 33
 34        return self.test(train_loader, device)
 35
 36 hdc_args = {"func": poison.hdc_dp,
 37            "scale_dot": 1,
```

```
38          "scale_norm": 10,
39          "labels": 10,
40          "one_d_len": 784,
41          "hdc_proj_len": 10000,
42          "view": [1, 28, 28]}
43
44  def hdc_train(hdc_data, device = 'cpu'):
45      hdc_data_loader = torch.utils.data.
            DataLoader(hdc_data, batch_size=len
46      (hdc_data), shuffle=True)
47      hdc_model = HDC(hdc_args["one_d_len"],
            hdc_args["hdc_proj_len"], len(hdc_args
48      ["labels"]), device)
49      train_acc = hdc_model.train(hdc_data_loader
            , device)
50      return hdc_model
51
52  hdc_clients_data = {client: (clients_data,
        hdc_train(clients_data))}
53
54  def hdc_dp(flip_labels, poison_percent,
        hdc_client_data):
55      data = hdc_client_data[0]
56      data = list(data)
57      mal_data = list()
58
59      train_vectors = hdc_client_data[1]
60      proj = hdc_client_data[2]
61      proj_inv = hdc_client_data[3]
62
63      for source_label, target_label in
            flip_labels.items():
64          b_arr = train_vectors[target_label]
65          norm_b = sim.norm(b_arr)
66          total_occurences = len([1 for _, label
                in data if label == source_label])
67          poison_count = poison_percent *
                total_occurences
68          if poison_percent == -1:
69              poison_count = total_occurences
70
```

```
label_poisoned = 0
for index, _ in enumerate(data):
    data[index] = list(data[index])

    if data[index][1] == source_label:
        img = data[index][0].reshape(1,
            hdc_args["one_d_len"])
        img_enc = sim.dot(img.detach().
            numpy(), proj.detach().numpy
            ())
        img_enc = torch.from_numpy(
            img_enc)

        c_arr = img_enc.reshape(
            hdc_args["hdc_proj_len"])
        p_arr = copy.deepcopy(c_arr)

        dot_mb = hdc_args["scale_dot"]
            * sim.dot(b_arr, c_arr)
        norm_c = sim.norm(c_arr)
        norm_m = norm_c
        sin_mg = 1

        kwargs = {"scale_norm":
            hdc_args["scale_norm"]} if
            "scale_norm" in hdc_args else
            {}

        for _index in range(3500):
            p_arr, dot_mb, norm_m,
                sim_mg, updated = sim.
                cosine_coord_vector_
                adapter(b_arr, p_arr,
                _index, dot_mb, norm_m,
                sim_mg, c_arr, norm_c,
                norm_b, **kwargs)

            if _index > 3470:
                _p_arr = p_arr.reshape
                    (1, hdc_args["
                    hdc_proj_len"])
```

```
97              p_img = sim.dot(_p_arr.
                    detach().numpy(),
                    proj_inv.detach().
                    numpy())
98              p_img = torch.
                    from_numpy(p_img)
99              p_img = p_img.view(
                    hdc_args["view"][0],
                    hdc_args["view
                    "][1], hdc_args["
                    view"][2])
100             sim.cosine_similarity(
                    data[index][0].view
                    (-1), p_img.view(-1)
                    ))
101             mal_data.append(tuple([
                    p_img, target_label
                    ]))
102
103             label_poisoned += 1
104
105             data[index] = tuple(data[index])
106
107             if label_poisoned >= poison_count:
108                 break
109
110     if poison_percent == -1:
111         return tuple(mal_data)
112
113     data = data + mal_data
114     return tuple(data)
```

## CHAPTER 4

Inference Attacks on FL

I N FL, CLIENTS SEND their local model updates to a central server without disclosing their raw training data. Even though FL aims to safeguard user privacy, sharing these local model updates could still pose significant privacy risks. As illustrated in Figure 4.1, an attacker can infer clients' private information by examining their model updates, for example, whether a patient has a specific disease. In this chapter, we focus on different inference attacks such as data reconstruction attacks, membership inference, and property inference attacks.

4.1 ATTACKER GOAL

The attacker aims to reconstruct sensitive information from the client's training dataset, unavailable to unauthorized parties. The attacker could be an honest-but-curious server (server-side attack) or a malicious client (client-side attack). In the case of a server-side attack, we assume that all the clients are honest. However, the server is interested in uncovering

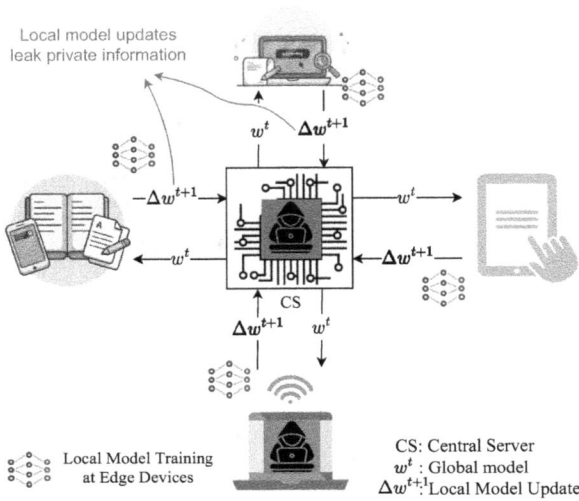

FIGURE 4.1   FL system under inference attacks.

the private information of the participating clients. On the other hand, for a client-side attack, we assume that the malicious client is a participant in FL and has its local dataset. Generally, the server is trustworthy and does not collaborate with the malicious client, who can receive the global model from the server.

The motivations for privacy attacks in FL can include:

- Access to Sensitive Information: Attackers may target FL systems to extract personal, medical, financial, or other sensitive data from local models or updates.

- Economic Gain: Corporations or individuals may seek to steal proprietary data or intellectual property (e.g., sensitive market data, trade secrets).

- Surveillance and Profiling: Governments or organizations may launch privacy attacks to profile users for political, marketing, or criminal surveillance.

- Model Stealing: Attackers may want to steal the underlying model's intellectual property by reverse engineering it through queries and updates.

- Bypassing Security Mechanisms: Attackers might aim to exploit FL to bypass centralized security controls (e.g., GDPR regulations, secure cloud environments), making decentralized attacks feasible.

- Competitive Advantage: Rival firms may launch privacy attacks to compromise competitor's data or models for industrial advantage.

4.2 DATA RECONSTRUCTION ATTACKS

Data reconstruction attacks aim to reconstruct other participants' local training examples precisely. A variety of data reconstruction attacks have been proposed in recent years [22, 30, 33, 67, 76, 82]. Following this, we will discuss one type of server-side data reconstruction attack, known as the DLG attack [82], as well as one client-side data reconstruction attack (GAN attack [30]).

4.2.1 DLG Attack

In the DLG attack [82], an honest-but-curious server employs data reconstruction techniques to reconstruct clients' private data. We use (x, y) to denote the reconstructed data, where x represents the feature vector and y is the corresponding label. The server aims to minimize the distance between the local model updates calculated with respect to (x, y) and the local model update of the targeted client. Specifically, the server first randomly initializes (x, y), then computes a local model update $\Delta w'$ at (x, y). Denote by Δw^t the targeted client's local model update. The server seeks to optimize (x, y) via solving the optimization problem:

$$x^*, y^* = \operatorname*{arg\,min}_{x,y} \left\| \Delta w' - \Delta w^t \right\|_2^2. \qquad (4.1)$$

The authors in [82] demonstrated that the DLG attack effectively reconstructs the training examples of the targeted client. Moreover, they showed that the server can initiate the attack during the training phase.

4.2.2 Hitaj Attack

Unlike the DLG attack described in [82], where an honest-but-curious server tries to reconstruct the clients' private data, the authors in [30] proposed a client-side data reconstruction attack in a collaborative environment. Specifically, in [30], the attacker is a participating client in FL and aims to infer private information about a label that belongs to another targeted client, which he or she does not possess. Specifically, the attacker performs the following steps in each training round to initiate the attack. First, the attacker downloads the current global model from the server. Next, the attacker uses a generative adversarial network (GAN) [25, 56] to generate similar training examples but labeled as a class that is not the target. The attacker then refines his or her local models using the augmented training data, which combines the attacker's original and the newly generated training examples. Finally, the attacker sends the updated local model back to the server. The authors in [30] showed that the GAN-based attack is effective if the targeted client aims to enhance its predictive accuracy. This remains true even when differential privacy [15] measures or sparsification [2] techniques are applied to the local models.

4.3 MEMBERSHIP INFERENCE ATTACKS

Membership inference attack aims to determine if a specific training example was used in the training process of a machine learning model [52, 55, 51].

4.3.1 Shokri Attack

Shokri *et al.* [61] proposed the first formal Membership Inference Attack (MIA) against machine learning models, where the adversary's goal is to determine whether a given private training data sample was part of the training dataset of a target model. This attack leverages the observation that models often behave differently on training data compared to unseen data. In particular, trained models tend to output higher confidence scores or lower loss values for data points they have seen during training, due to potential overfitting.

To exploit this behavior, the authors designed a two-stage attack. First, the attacker trains multiple *shadow models* that mimic the behavior of the target model. Each shadow model is trained on a known dataset partitioned into training and testing subsets. By querying these models, the attacker collects prediction vectors (e.g., softmax outputs) for both training data (labeled as "in") and testing data (labeled as "out") to build an *attack dataset*. This dataset consists of input features as model prediction vectors and binary labels indicating membership status. Second, an *attack model* is trained on this constructed dataset to distinguish between "in" and "out" samples based on their prediction behaviors. Once trained, this attack model can be used to infer the membership status of arbitrary samples with respect to the target model by analyzing its prediction output.

This work demonstrated that models trained with standard techniques (especially deep learning models) are vulnerable to MIAs, even when only limited (black-box) access (e.g., prediction API) is available. The study also initiated a line of research into privacy risks in machine learning and provided a foundational attack model that many subsequent membership inference strategies extend or build upon.

4.3.2 Nasr Attack

Nasr *et al.* [52] demonstrated a comprehensive analysis of white-box membership inference attacks in both centralized (standalone) and federated learning settings. Unlike black-box attacks, which rely only on the output predictions of the target model, their approach assumes white-box access to the model (the ability to inspect internal parameters, activations, and gradients). In the centralized setup, the adversary monitors the trained target model and observes how it changes when updated with additional data; this allows the attacker to correlate model behavior in the presence of particular samples. In the federated setting, the server has access to the local model updates submitted by clients, which can be exploited to infer sensitive information. Similarly, a malicious client may observe the global model across rounds and analyze it to extract membership information.

The authors design an attack model that takes as input both the data sample (to be investigated) and the target model (with white-box access). The attack pipeline captures the entire computation of the target model on the input, including intermediate representations. Specifically, the forward pass outputs (activations, prediction vector, and loss) are fed into a fully connected neural network (FCN), while the gradients from the backward pass are passed through a convolutional neural network (CNN). They capture complementary information about how the target model processes the input. Their outputs are then concatenated and passed into an encoder-decoder network, where the encoder output is used to make the final membership inference. This work demonstrates that having white-box access significantly increases the efficacy of membership inference attacks, revealing deeper vulnerabilities in training pipelines.

4.3.3 Zhang Attack

The work by Zhang *et al.* [79] demonstrates a powerful membership inference attack (MIA) in federated learning (FL) using generative adversarial networks (GANs). In this attack, an adversarial client participating in FL locally constructs a GAN to approximate the distribution of the training data held by other benign clients. The attacker then queries the global model with the generated synthetic data to obtain corresponding labels, effectively creating a labeled dataset. This labeled data is used to train a membership inference classifier that distinguishes whether a particular sample was part of the training data of the global model. The attack proceeds, with the GAN and classifier being updated during each communication round of FL. Notably, the attack does not rely on the global model being overfitted, challenging a common assumption behind many prior MIAs. Furthermore, the authors highlight that even with privacy-preserving techniques such as dropout or input noise, the inference attack remains effective, emphasizing the inherent vulnerability of FL to data leakage via generative modeling and adversarial training.

4.4 PROPERTY INFERENCE ATTACK

Sometimes, the attacker is interested in inferring about a sensitive property other than the main classification task. Suppose the target model is trained for male-female classification. Ideally, the model should only learn to discriminate between male and female. However, due to its complex nature, it also learns irrelevant features, which may be sensitive and interesting for an adversary. Authors in [65] classify property inference attacks into (1) class sniffing, (2) quantity inference, and (3) whole determination attack. In a class sniffing attack, the attacker is interested in whether a particular class label is present in the private dataset of the target model. In a quantity inference attack, the attacker is interested in the amount (quantity) of the class label in the private training dataset. In the whole determination attack, the attacker determines the presence of a sensitive property, which the target model was not intended to reveal.

4.4.1 MILSA: Model Interpretation-Based Label Sniffing Attack in Federated Learning

Authors in [48] proposed a property inference attack employing a model interpretation technique (using Shapley value) to infer the presence of class label and its quantity in the private training dataset on which the target model was trained.

They proposed an attack model, which takes the target model and a few auxiliary data as input. The model interpreter technique using Shapley gives feature importance (attribution scores) to any input image for the given target model. These attribution scores are matrices of input image size for each label. For example, in an MNIST model, the model interpreter returns an output of 10 matrices, each of size 28×28. Then, MILSA performs operations over these matrices to learn the presence of label composition in the private training dataset. Each attribution score matrix is converted to one dimension and summed up to obtain a single value. Thus, we get n scalar values for a n-label classification model. After that, employing z-score over these values, the outlier can be detected if the z-score is more significant than 3σ or smaller than -3σ, which implies that the particular label was not present. Similarly, if the z-score is larger than 2σ or smaller than -2σ, the particular label was partially present. Suppose the score is more centered around the mean. In that case, the probability of the presence of a particular label is high and equal to any other label present in the private training dataset.

4.4.2 MIPIA: Model Interpretation-Based Property Inference Attack

The authors extended MILSA to present a property inference attack employing the model interpretation technique. Most existing attacks employ shadow models and meta-classifiers to train on auxiliary data with and without property. On the contrary, MIPIA saves the effort of training more models; instead, it interprets the model only with the knowledge of very few samples with and without property. A property inference attack aims to detect property in the private training dataset. MIPIA is tailored with a unique feature that infers the presence of property for each label in the main classification task. For example, in a male-female classification model, existing attacks are framed to learn the presence of a property like wearing sunglasses or smiling (open mouth) over the whole training dataset. This is also because of the fundamental nature of the attacks, which relies on training shadow models with and without property over the complete data distribution. Meanwhile, MIPIA can infer the presence of property for both males and females.

MIPIA frames an attack model that inputs the target model and auxiliary data with and without property. The model interpreter first takes the target model and the input data with the property as input and outputs the attribution matrices, as discussed in MILSA. Similarly, it takes the target model and the input data without property as input and outputs the attribution matrices. Both these attribution matrices are operated to achieve label-wise property inference. The intuition behind the attack is that a model learns to classify the main task based on the discriminatory features. Suppose a model is trained with males only wearing sunglasses and females without sunglasses. Here, sunglasses become a discriminatory feature. Thus, the difference in attribution scores in the region of sunglasses will reveal this information. However, the limitation of this attack is that it can not be learned if the properties are mostly not present in the region of interest.

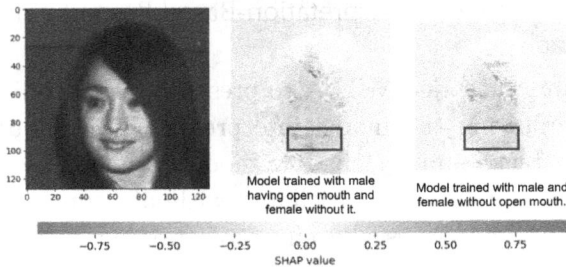

FIGURE 4.2 Model interpretation for slightly open mouth attribute.

Figure 4.2 illustrates model interpretation analysis on two target models: (1) a male with a slightly open mouth and a female without it; (2) a male and female without a slightly open mouth against a female with a closed mouth. It can be observed that attributions near the mouth are darker (they actually look red and denote positive attributions) (1), as the target model (f) has not seen a female with open mouth, and lighter (actually look gray and denote neutral) in (2), as f has only seen male or female with closed mouth, so this property is irrelevant for f.

4.5 IMPLEMENTATION

4.5.1 Data Reconstruction Attack

We present an implementation code for DLG attack, which can be extended further for other data reconstruction attacks.

```
class SimpleMLP(nn.Module):
    def __init__(self, input_dim=2, hidden_dim
        =32, output_dim=2):
        super().__init__()
        self.net = nn.Sequential(
            nn.Linear(input_dim, hidden_dim),
            nn.ReLU(),
            nn.Linear(hidden_dim, output_dim)
        )
```

```
        def forward(self, x):
            return self.net(x)


def get_real_data():
    x_real = torch.tensor([[2.0, -1.0]],
        requires_grad=False)
    y_real = torch.tensor([1], dtype=torch.
    long)
    return x_real, y_real


def get_real_gradients(model, x_real, y_real):
    model.zero_grad()
    loss = nn.CrossEntropyLoss()(model(x_real),
        y_real)
    loss.backward()
    return [p.grad.clone().detach() for p in
        model.parameters()]


def dlg_attack(target_model, real_grads, iters
    =300, lr=0.1):
    # Initialize dummy input and label
    dummy_x = torch.randn((1, 2), requires_grad
        =True)
    dummy_y_logits = torch.randn((1, 2),
        requires_grad=True)  # logits to softmax

    optimizer = optim.Adam([dummy_x,
        dummy_y_logits], lr=lr)

    for i in range(iters):
        optimizer.zero_grad()

        # Compute dummy loss
        dummy_y_prob = torch.softmax(
            dummy_y_logits, dim=-1)
        dummy_y = torch.argmax(dummy_y_prob,
            dim=1)
```

```
pred = target_model(dummy_x)
loss = nn.CrossEntropyLoss()(pred,
    dummy_y)

# Get dummy gradients
target_model.zero_grad()
loss.backward()
dummy_grads = [p.grad.clone() for p in
    target_model.parameters()]

# Compute gradient matching loss (L2)
grad_diff = 0
for real_g, dummy_g in zip(real_grads,
    dummy_grads):
        grad_diff += ((real_g - dummy_g) **
            2).sum()

grad_diff.backward()
optimizer.step()

if i % 50 == 0 or i == iters - 1:
        print(f"Iter {i}: Grad matching
            loss = {grad_diff.item():.4f}")

    # Return reconstructed data
    reconstructed_x = dummy_x.detach()
    reconstructed_y = torch.argmax(torch.
        softmax(dummy_y_logits, dim=-1), dim=1).
        item()
    return reconstructed_x, reconstructed_y

def run_dlg():
    model = SimpleMLP()
    x_real, y_real = get_real_data()
    real_grads = get_real_gradients(model,
        x_real, y_real)

    # Perform the DLG attack
    x_rec, y_rec = dlg_attack(model,
        real_grads)
```

```
75    print("\nOriginal x:", x_real)
76    print("Reconstructed x:", x_rec)
77    print("Original y:", y_real.item())
78    print("Reconstructed y:", y_rec)
```

4.5.2 Membership Inference Attack

We present implementation code for MIA, which can be further extended for other MIAs.

```
1   class TargetModel(nn.Module):
2       def __init__(self, input_dim, hidden_dim
            =64):
3           super().__init__()
4           self.net = nn.Sequential(
5               nn.Linear(input_dim, hidden_dim),
6               nn.ReLU(),
7               nn.Linear(hidden_dim, 2)  # Binary
                    classification
8           )
9
10      def forward(self, x):
11          return self.net(x)
12
13  class AttackModel(nn.Module):
14      def __init__(self):
15          super().__init__()
16          self.net = nn.Sequential(
17              nn.Linear(1, 32),
18              nn.ReLU(),
19              nn.Linear(32, 1),
20              nn.Sigmoid()  # Outputs membership
                    probability
21          )
22
23      def forward(self, x):
24          return self.net(x)
25
26
```

```
def train_model(model, data_loader, criterion,
    optimizer, epochs=10):
    model.train()
    for epoch in range(epochs):
        for xb, yb in data_loader:
            optimizer.zero_grad()
            out = model(xb)
            loss = criterion(out.squeeze(), yb)
            loss.backward()
            optimizer.step()


def extract_confidence(model, data_loader):
    model.eval()
    confidences = []
    with torch.no_grad():
        for xb, yb in data_loader:
            logits = model(xb)
            probs = torch.softmax(logits, dim
                =1)
            true_probs = probs.gather(1, yb.
                view(-1, 1)).squeeze()
            confidences.append(true_probs.view
                (-1, 1))  # Shape:
                [batch_size, 1]
    return torch.cat(confidences, dim=0)


def run_mia():
    # Generate synthetic data
    num_samples = 2000
    input_dim = 20

    X = torch.randn(num_samples, input_dim)
    y = torch.randint(0, 2, (num_samples,))

    # Split data for training and testing the
        target model
    X_train, X_test, y_train, y_test =
        train_test_split(X, y, test_size=0.5)
```

```
# Create data loaders
train_loader = DataLoader(TensorDataset(
    X_train, y_train), batch_size=64,
    shuffle=True)
test_loader = DataLoader(TensorDataset(
    X_test, y_test), batch_size=64)

# Step 1: Train the target model
target_model = TargetModel(input_dim)
criterion = nn.CrossEntropyLoss()
optimizer = optim.Adam(target_model.
    parameters(), lr=0.001)
train_model(target_model, train_loader,
    criterion, optimizer, epochs=10)

# Step 2: Extract confidence scores for
    training and test samples
in_confidences = extract_confidence(
    target_model, train_loader)  # "in"
    samples
out_confidences = extract_confidence(
    target_model, test_loader)  # "out"
    samples

# Step 3: Prepare attack dataset
X_attack = torch.cat([in_confidences,
    out_confidences], dim=0)
y_attack = torch.cat([
    torch.ones(in_confidences.size(0)),  #
        label 1: in training
    torch.zeros(out_confidences.size(0))  #
        label 0: not in training
])

attack_dataset = TensorDataset(X_attack,
    y_attack)
attack_loader = DataLoader(attack_dataset,
    batch_size=64, shuffle=True)

# Step 4: Train the attack model
attack_model = AttackModel()
```

```
attack_criterion = nn.BCELoss()
attack_optimizer = optim.Adam(attack_model.
    parameters(), lr=0.001)
train_model(attack_model, attack_loader,
    attack_criterion, attack_optimizer,
    epochs=10)

# Step 5: Evaluate attack model accuracy
attack_model.eval()
with torch.no_grad():
    preds = attack_model(X_attack).squeeze
        ()
    predicted_labels = (preds >= 0.5).float
        ()
    acc = (predicted_labels == y_attack).
        float().mean().item()
    print("Attack Accuracy: {acc * 100:.2f
        }% - Ability to infer membership!")
```

4.5.3 Property Inference Attack

We present the above-discussed MIPIA (Model Interpretation-Based Property Inference Attack).

4.5.3.1 Prepare Auxiliary Dataset

```
df = pd.read_csv('../../data/attr_celeba/
    list_attr_celeba.txt', sep="\s+", skiprows
    =1, usecols=['Male', 'Smiling'])
df.loc[df['Male'] == -1, 'Male'] = 0

male_s = df[(df.Male==1) & (df.Smiling == 1)
    ][:10]
male_ns = df[(df.Male==1) & (df.Smiling == -1)
    ][:10]
female_s = df[(df.Male==0) & (df.Smiling == 1)
    ][:10]
female_ns = df[(df.Male==0) & (df.Smiling ==
    -1)][:10]
```

```
male_s.to_csv('male_s.csv')
male_ns.to_csv('male_ns.csv')
female_s.to_csv('female_s.csv')
female_ns.to_csv('female_ns.csv')


train_male_s_dataset = CelebaDataset(csv_path='
    male_s.csv', img_dir='../../data/celeba/
    img_align_celeba/', transform=
    custom_transform)


train_male_ns_dataset = CelebaDataset(csv_path
    ='male_ns.csv', img_dir='../../data/celeba/
    img_align_celeba/', transform=
    custom_transform)


train_female_s_dataset = CelebaDataset(csv_path
    ='female_s.csv', img_dir='../../data/celeba/
    img_align_celeba/', transform=
    custom_transform)


train_female_ns_dataset = CelebaDataset(
    csv_path='female_ns.csv', img_dir='../../
    data/celeba/img_align_celeba/', transform=
    custom_transform)


train_male_s_loader = DataLoader(dataset=
    train_male_s_dataset, batch_size=BATCH_SIZE,
    shuffle=True, num_workers=0)


train_male_ns_loader = DataLoader(dataset=
    train_male_ns_dataset, batch_size=BATCH_SIZE
    , shuffle=True, num_workers=0)
```

```
33  train_female_s_loader = DataLoader(dataset=
        train_female_s_dataset, batch_size=
        BATCH_SIZE, shuffle=True, num_workers=0)
34
35  train_female_ns_loader = DataLoader(dataset=
        train_female_ns_dataset, batch_size=
        BATCH_SIZE, shuffle=True, num_workers=0)
36
37  print(len(train_female_ns_loader))
38
39  target_fns_batch = next(iter(
        train_female_ns_loader))
40  target_fns_images, _ = target_fns_batch
41
42  target_fs_batch = next(iter(
        train_female_s_loader))
43  target_fs_images, _ = target_fs_batch
44
45  target_mns_batch = next(iter(
        train_male_ns_loader))
46  target_mns_images, _ = target_mns_batch
47
48  target_ms_batch = next(iter(train_male_s_
49  loader))
50  target_ms_images, _ = target_ms_batch
```

4.5.3.2 Attribution Scores in the Region of Interest

```
1  target_shap_values = shap_plot(target_explain,
       reference_img, 49152)
2  target_female = torch.tensor(target_shap_values
       [0]).view(-1)
3  target_male = torch.tensor(target_shap_values
       [1]).view(-1)
4
5  target_female_crop = torch.tensor(
       target_shap_values[0][0:1, 0:3, 80:120,
       40:80]).view(-1)
6  target_male_crop = torch.tensor(
       target_shap_values[1][0:1, 0:3, 80:120,
       40:80]).view(-1)
```

4.5.3.3 Operation Over Attribution Scores Helps to Infer Properties

```
target_explain = shap.DeepExplainer(
    target_model, target_baseline)


for smile_female_img in range(2,10):
    target_image = target_fs_images[
        smile_female_img]
    r_img = target_image
    target_shap_values = shap_plot(
        target_explain, r_img, 49152)
    target_female = torch.tensor(
        target_shap_values[0]).view(-1)
    #target_male = torch.tensor(
        target_shap_values[1]).view(-1)


    target_smile_female_crop = torch.tensor(
        target_shap_values[0][0:1, 0:3, 80:120,
        40:80]).view(-1)
    #target_male_crop = torch.tensor(
        target_shap_values[1][0:1, 0:3, 80:120,
        40:80]).view(-1)


    for non_smile_female_img in range(10):
        target_image = target_fns_images[
            non_smile_female_img]
        r_img = target_image
        target_shap_values = shap_plot(
            target_explain, r_img, 49152)
        target_female = torch.tensor(
            target_shap_values[0]).view(-1)
        #target_male = torch.tensor(
            target_shap_values[1]).view(-1)


        target_non_smile_female_crop = torch.
            tensor(target_shap_values[0][0:1,
            0:3, 80:120, 40:80]).view(-1)
```

```
25    #target_male_crop = torch.tensor(
         target_shap_values[1][0:1, 0:3,
         80:120, 40:80]).view(-1)
26
27    res = sum(target_non_smile_female_crop
         - target_smile_female_crop)
28    print(res)
```

## CHAPTER 5

Byzantine-Robust Defenses

$\mathbf{B}$YZANTINE FAILURES HAVE BEEN largely ignored by distributed machine learning frameworks. These failures may occur unintentionally due to software bugs, hardware failures, and network issues, as well as intentionally in the presence of malicious participants aiming to degrade overall model performance. Existing studies investigated such vulnerabilities and proposed various Byzantine-robust defenses. Since clients have the independence to store a local, unseen data partition that may not necessarily satisfy the global learning objective. The central server cannot easily determine whether a gradient indicates a malicious objective. Only a small subset of the original dataset and the stochastic objective changes are used during each iteration. Hence, a sporadic update cannot be considered malicious by the aggregator. With decreasing batch size b, the variance of client updates increases. When sampling a smaller portion of the dataset, gradient values have a higher variance, resulting in sporadic behavior. Thus, it becomes challenging to detect a malicious client.

DOI: 10.1201/9781003688570-5

5.1 DESIGN GOAL

The performance of federated learning should be preserved when the system is not attacked. Client contributions pointing in the same direction should be devalued. An increasing number of Sybil should not pose a problem. It should differentiate between honest updates that mistakenly appear malicious due to SGD variance and Sybil updates that act in the same malicious manner. There should be no reliance on external assumptions about the number of clients or the model type. We list some more design goals below:

1. *Mitigation of Poisoning Attack:* The defense technique should mitigate the attack by restricting the attack success rate/attack impact to a no-attack scenario.

2. *Integrity of FL Cycle:* The defense technique should not make any changes to the default FL training cycle. It should be similar to a no-attack scenario.

3. *Fewer Assumptions and Knowledge:* There should not be any strong assumptions or knowledge, like white-box access of deep neural network model, number of attackers, or any extra configuration and calibration.

Let us discuss a very preliminary Euclidean-based defense. Suppose there are five participants and each of them owns a digit. We have to find the outlier among them based on the sum of the Euclidean distance.

$$P_1 : 1, P_2 : 2, P_3 : 2, P_4 : 1, P_5 : 5$$

Now, the sum of the Euclidean distance from each participant to the remaining is calculated as follows:

From P_1 to remaining $:(0 + 1 + 1 + 0 + 16), i.e., 18$

From P_2 to remaining $:(1 + 0 + 0 + 1 + 9), i.e., 11$

From P_3 to remaining :$(1 + 0 + 0 + 1 + 9)$, *i.e.*, 11

From P_4 to remaining :$(0 + 1 + 1 + 0 + 16)$, *i.e.*, 18

From P_5 to remaining :$(16 + 9 + 9 + 16 + 0)$, *i.e.*, 40

Here, it can be easily noticed that P_5 is a malicious participant. Now, if P_5 adds a sybil P_6 : 5.

$$P_1 : 1, P_2 : 2. P_3 : 2, P_4 : 1, P_5 : 5, P_6 : 5$$

Now, the updated sum of the Euclidean distance from each participant to the remaining is calculated as follows:

From P_1 to remaining :$(0 + 1 + 1 + 0 + 16 + 16)$, *i.e.*, 34

From P_2 to remaining :$(1 + 0 + 0 + 1 + 9 + 9)$, *i.e.*, 20

From P_3 to remaining :$(1 + 0 + 0 + 1 + 9 + 9)$, *i.e.*, 20

From P_4 to remaining :$(0 + 1 + 1 + 0 + 16 + 16)$, *i.e.*, 34

From P_5 and P_6 to remaining :$(16 + 9 + 9 + 16 + 0 + 0)$, *i.e.*, 40

Here, it can be noticed that Byzantine workers pull the mean toward themselves. The problem with this approach is that it involves all vectors, even those far away. A single Byzantine worker makes the mean to approach itself by proposing large enough vectors.

Thus, no gradient aggregation rule can tolerate a single Byzantine failure based on a linear combination of the vectors proposed by the workers. A linear combination of gradients gives the adversary full control of the aggregated gradient (model parameters). In a non linear, squared-distance-based aggregation rule, the vector with the smallest sum of squared distances to every other vector is selected as the vector closest to the barycenter. Despite this, a squared-distance aggregation rule only tolerates a single Byzantine worker. A pair of Byzantine workers can collude, helping the second by moving their barycenters away from the "correct area".

Now, we discuss state-of-the-art byzantine-robust defenses.

5.2 KRUM

Krum [8] satisfies a Byzantine resilience property, which guarantees convergence despite m malicious participants out of n participants.

5.2.1 Byzantine Resilience Property

The primary criterion to be fulfilled by any algorithm should be that: (1) The chosen output vector should point to the average; (2) Statistical moments (up to the fourth moment) bounded above by a homogeneous polynomial in the moments of a correct estimator of the gradient. This property can be achieved using a majority-based approach, finding the subset with the smallest diameter and considering every subset of $n - m$ vectors.

Using both majority-based and squared-distance-based approaches, Krum finds the vector closest to $n - m$ vectors. Krum satisfies the byzantine-resilience property, given $2m + 2 < n$. The local time complexity of Krum is $O(n^2.d)$, where d is the dimension of parameter space of the gradient.

As discussed earlier, a single Byzantine participant makes the barycenter move toward itself. Thus, Krum precludes such vectors that are far away. For each participant P_i which owns an update U_i, the score is calculated as:

$$s(U_i) = \sum_{i \to j}^{n-m-2} ||U_i - U_j||^2$$

where j runs over the closest $n - m - 2$ updates. Finally, Krum selects an update k, such that $s(U_k) \leq s(u_i)$, for all i.

However, Krum pays the cost of resilience, as learning slows down when there is no Byzantine participant. This overhead can be reduced by increasing the batch size.

5.2.2 Multi-Krum

It is a Krum variant that calculates scores like Krum. However, it selects a subset of participants (maximum $n - m$ participants) with the best scores and averages them.

5.3 MEDIAN AND TRIMMED-MEAN

These are provably robust distributed gradient descent algorithms based on median and trimmed mean [74] operations, respectively. These algorithms achieve order-optimal statistical error rates for strongly convex losses.

In a distributed machine learning setting, we expect the error rate to decrease with a larger data kn (where k is the number of data points owned by each client) and a reduced fraction of attackers (α). Still, the error rate cannot be less than:

$$\widetilde{\Omega} \left(\frac{\alpha}{\sqrt{k}} + \frac{1}{\sqrt{kn}} \right) = \widetilde{\Omega} \left(\frac{1}{\sqrt{k}} \left(\alpha + \frac{1}{\sqrt{n}} \right) \right) \qquad (5.1)$$

As long as there are no or few Byzantine machines, the usual scaling of $\frac{1}{\sqrt{kn}}$ is observed; when some Byzantine machines exist, their influence remains bounded and proportional to α. If any algorithm guarantees this bound, then no extra cost is being paid, as this is unavoidable.

While guaranteeing robustness, from Byzantine failures, communication efficiency should also be taken care of. Thus, the minimum communication should be made and that should not be greater than the dimension of the parameter space ($O(d)$) of the local model update of any participant.

Coordinate-wise median: The global model is calculated as $g := med\{x^i : i \in n\}$, where each coordinate k is calculated as: $g_k = med\{x_k^i : i \in n\}$, for each $k \in [d]$, med is the one-dimensional (statistical) median operation.

Coordinate-wise trimmed mean: Given $\beta \in [0, \frac{1}{2})$ (set of Byzantine participants), the global model is calculated as $g := trmean_\beta \{x^i : i \in n\}$, where each coordinate k is calculated as: $g_k = \frac{1}{(1-2\beta)n} \sum_{x \in U_k} x$, for each $k \in [d]$, U_k is the subset of $\{x_k^1, x_k^2, ..., x_k^p\}$, after removing the smallest and largest β fraction of elements.

5.4 BULYAN

Bulyan [26] contradicts the above-claimed guarantees of Byzantine resilience in the presence of a minority of adversaries. It shows that convergence is not enough. Given $d \gg 1$, an attacker can make use of the non-convexity of the loss function such that the global model converges to ineffective models. This work highlights that existing Byzantine-resilient algorithms still leave a margin of poisoning of $\Omega(f(d))$, where $f(d)$ increases at least like $\sqrt{d}$. Bulyan reduces this margin to $O(\frac{1}{\sqrt{d}})$.

In the threat model, the adversary is assumed to be omniscient and has complete system knowledge. However, the adversary is not omnipotent; it can only submit compromised updates from m malicious participants.

Bulyan ensures both convergence and guarantee on each coordinate being selected after being agreed upon by most participants, using a byzantine-resilient algorithm $\mathcal{A}$. $\mathcal{A}$ can be any algorithm like Krum, based on the Euclidean norm. Bulyan requires $n \geq 4m + 3$ gradients. In the first step, using $\mathcal{A}$ (Krum), the best gradient is selected, removed from the original set, and added to a selection set S. Repeat this process, till $|S| < \theta$, where $n \geq 4m + 3$ and $\theta = n - 2m \geq 2m + 3$.

Now, the set S contains the majority of honest participants. Further, for each coordinate $i \in [d]$, the median of gradients in S at i is bounded by honest gradients. In the second step, each coordinate i of the resulting gradient is calculated as the average of β closest i-th coordinates to the median i-th coordinate of gradients from S, where $\beta = \theta - 2m \geq 3$.

The computational cost of one Bulyan aggregation, using Krum, is $O(n^2 d)$.

5.5 FOOLSGOLD

FoolsGold [20] studies the effect of model poisoning and highlights the added risk in case of Sybil-based poisoning attacks. It identifies the increased vulnerabilities caused by poisoning sybils based on the diversity of client updates. In FL, all participants have almost equal influence (weight), which makes sybils overpower a system, even with a majority of honest participants. The influence is generally decided based on the number of samples held with a client, which a malicious participant can easily adjust. It is observed that Multi-Krum can defend only up to 33% poisoning sybils.

It also highlights the challenge associated with SGD, as detecting malicious behavior from the SGD (Stochastic gradient descent) stream becomes more difficult compared to GD (Gradient descent). The major challenges associated with SGD are: (1) Clients have their own local, unseen partitions of data that may not satisfy the global learning objective, making it difficult for the aggregator to determine whether the gradient is malicious. (2) The stochastic objective changes in each iteration since only a small portion of the training dataset is used for training. Therefore, it becomes difficult for the aggregator to determine whether gradients pointing in sporadic directions are malicious or gradients pointing in similar directions are from similar datasets. (3) With decreasing batch size, the variance of submitted gradients increases. This allows adversaries to submit arbitrary gradients, as no specific batch size configuration is defined.

The motivation behind FoolsGold's design is that the gradient updates of honest clients are more diverse than those of sybils. Since honest clients share unique distribution, the sybils share a common objective. FoolsGold maintains the clients' learning rate, giving unique updates while modifying the learning rates of sybils. It also considers the past reputation of clients.

FoolsGold uses cosine similarity measures to find similarities among clients' submitted updates. It is easier to modify Euclidean distance to achieve dissimilarity than cosine similarity. Further, FoolsGold takes feature importance into account while measuring cosine similarity. Three types of features exist in a model: (1) relevant features both for the model and attack, (2) relevant features required for the correctness of the model but irrelevant to an attack, and (3) irrelevant features both for the model and attack. Thus, the similarity is measured between the relevant features (1 and 2). This also restricts Sybils from manipulating irrelevant features for achieving dissimilarity. Such features (1 and 2) can be estimated by looking at the magnitude of the model parameters in the output layer. This is because these parameters directly influence the prediction probabilities. Such features are filtered and normalized across all classes to avoid biasing one class over the other. FoolsGold also takes the clients' past reputation by individually aggregating the updates in each iteration.

5.5.1 Defense Execution

First, the pairwise cosine similarity score (cs_{ij}) among participants i and j is calculated between their aggregated gradients. The cosine similarity score is in the range of -1 to 1. Then, v_i is the maximum pairwise similarity for client i. As discussed, cosine similarity cannot be the strong similarity measure because sybils can also produce diverse gradients harnessing SGD. This may punish the honest participants. So, FoolsGold introduces a pardoning mechanism. For each score v_i, if $v_j > v_i$, the pairwise cosine similarity score is reweighted as $cs_{ij}* = \frac{v_i}{v_j}$. Then, the updated learning rate (α_i) is calculated as $1 - max(cs_{ij})$. Here, the learning rate is rescaled between 0 and 1, such that at least one honest client gets a score of 1. It is still possible that a few similar gradients possess a cosine similarity score of less than one. This can be exploited by sybils. Consequently, FoolsGold promotes a higher divergence and avoids penalizing honest clients for low similarity scores. So, it uses the logit function to rescale the learning rate (α_i) as,

$$\alpha_i = \kappa \left(\ln \left[\frac{\alpha_i}{1 - \alpha_i} \right] + 0.5 \right), \qquad (5.2)$$

where K is a confidence parameter that can be set as a data distribution function to guarantee convergence. Further, α_i is clipped if exceeding the range of 0–1.

5.5.2 Adaptive Attack Analysis

If the attackers (sybils) try to maintain higher divergence between the submitted updates, they will deviate from their objective of poisoning. Thus, there exists a tradeoff between lower detection and lower attack.

Another approach to frame adaptive attack is adding intelligent noise to a pair of gradients, such that their sum becomes zero. This attack can also be framed with more than two sybils by introducing orthogonal noise vectors so that their sum reaches zero. However, adding noise in such a way does not fulfill any poisoning objective and increases the chances of getting detected because of Sybil dissimilarity.

5.6 FLTRUST

The above-discussed Byzantine-robust defenses perform statistical analysis to identify outliers among the client's submitted updates. However, a scope still exists to craft malicious updates by carefully poisoning models [18]. This is because there does not exist any root of trust with the central server. FLTrust [11] addresses this issue by bootstrapping trust at the central server. To bootstrap trust, the central server collects a small (clean) training dataset and trains a central model over it. Then, the central server assigns a trust score to each client in reference to the server update. The trust score is calculated based on the direction and magnitude of the submitted updates. The updates similar to the server model update get a high trust score and vice versa. Further, FLTrust performs normalization operations on the submitted updates to limit the effect to large or small magnitudes.

5.6.1 Trust Score

The attacker perturbs direction to poison the model. With the trusted server update trained by the central server, FLTrust needs to detect the poisoned model. The submitted updates, with a more similar direction to the trusted server update, are considered more benign. FLTrust uses cosine similarity to measure the direction similarity between the client's local model update and trusted server update. Cosine similarity (c_i) is calculated as $\frac{<g_i,g_0>}{||g_i||.||g_0||}$, where w_i is the client's local model update and g_0 is the trusted server update and $||.||$ is the magnitude (l_2 norm) of local model update. Further, the trust score (TS) is calculated as $ReLU(c_i)$. $ReLU$ is used to clip negative local model updates in the opposite direction to the trusted server update. Thus, $ReLU(c_i) = c_i$, if $c_i > 0$, else $ReLU(c_i) = 0$.

5.6.2 Normalization

The client's local model updates have different magnitudes, larger or smaller than the trusted server update. Thus, each update needs to be normalized with respect to the trusted server update as $\bar{g}_i = \frac{||g_0||}{||g_i||}.g_i$. Normalization rescales the local model updates such that all the updates lie on the same vector space. It ensures that all the submitted updates have a similar impact on the aggregation.

5.6.3 Aggregation

The global model is calculated as the weighted average of normalized updates using the trust scores, as stated in Equation 5.3.

$$g = \frac{1}{\sum_{j=1}^{n} TS_j} \sum_{i=1}^{n} TS_i \cdot \bar{g}_i$$

$$= \frac{1}{\sum_{j=1}^{n} \text{ReLU}(c_j)} \sum_{i=1}^{n} \text{ReLU}(c_i) \cdot \frac{\|g_0\|}{\|g_i\|} \cdot g_i \qquad (5.3)$$

Finally, the global model for the next iteration is calculated as $w \leftarrow w - \alpha.g$, where α is the global learning rate.

5.7 MOAT

Moat [47] stands for **Mo**del **A**gnostic Defense against **T**argeted Poisoning Attacks in Federated Learning. The state-of-the-art defenses based on statistical similarity suffer from a large number of attackers or an ingenious technique for injecting backdoor noise. Moat measures individual features' marginal contributions using interpretation techniques. Detection of an adversary relies on aggregating interpreted values against a baseline input. Moat is robust to adversarial noise in homogeneous or heterogeneous distributions, regardless of the number of attackers. Moat achieves model convergence despite 90% attackers, which is its most appealing feature.

5.7.1 Overview

Moat uses the Shapley algorithm to calculate individual feature attributions (ϕ_i) for interpreting the predictions. It assigns an important score to each feature value with all possible coalitions for a particular prediction. Equation 5.4 explains the calculation using a value function, where S is the selected set of features, x is the data vector selected for interpretation, and p is the number of features considered.

$$\phi_j(\text{val}) = \sum_{S \subseteq [x_1, \dots, x_p] \setminus (x_j)} \frac{|S|!(p - |S| - 1)!}{p!} \, (\text{val}\,(S \cup \{x_1\})$$

$$- \text{val}(S)) \tag{5.4}$$

$val_x(S)$ is the prediction for the feature values in set S, marginalized over features not included in the set S. It is demonstrated in Equation 5.5 and is calculated through multiple integrations.

$$\text{val}_x(S) = \int \hat{f}(x_1, \dots, x_p) \, dP_{x \notin S} - E_X(\hat{f}(X)) \tag{5.5}$$

Figure 5.1 illustrates feature attributions (Shapley value) when an image is given input to a benign and poisoned model. f is a benign model trained over a homogeneous distribution of the handwritten digit (MNIST) dataset. f' is a poisoned model trained over a label-flipped dataset (where "4" is labeled as "9"). It can be observed that given image "4" in f, the distribution of darker (they actually look red and denote positive attributions) attributions is at the correct place (label "4"), while in f', the distribution of positive (red) attributions is at the wrong place (flipped label "9").

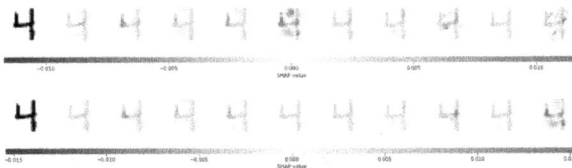

FIGURE 5.1   Feature attributions in a benign (f) and malign model (f').

5.7.2 Detection of Poisoned Clients and Labels

Moat takes the submitted updates and a few clean samples from a similar distribution (reference data) as input. Then, it uses Shapley to interpret the model, using the model and reference data. It also takes an image as input for interpretation. The input image can be either a real or zero-vector (blank) image. For example, Figures 5.2 and 5.3 illustrate the feature attributions using a black image over f and f'. f' is trained over poisoned data, where the model misclassifies label "2" images in the presence of a trigger. It can be observed that, when compared to the benign model spectrum, the attacked label shows a mostly negative spectrum.

As shown in Figures 5.1–5.3, Shapley returns feature attributions for all labels on which a given model is trained. Each attribution value may fall in positive, negative, or zero values. Moat sums up all the attributions for each label, which results in an array of length equal to the number of labels. Next, Moat detects the outliers over the sum of attributions using Z-score. For each instance, x in the array, Z-score is calculated as $\frac{x-\mu}{\sigma}$, where μ is the mean and σ is the standard deviation of the array. A threshold is defined based on application sensitivity.

FIGURE 5.2   Benign model f (feature attributions over a zero-vector image).

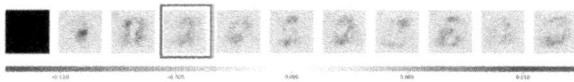

FIGURE 5.3   Poisoned model f' (feature attributions over a zero-vector image).

If any instance x exceeds the threshold, the label is attacked. Hence, the corresponding client is considered to be malicious.

5.8 DeFL

DeFL [70] stands for *Defending Against Model Poisoning Attacks in Federated Learning via Critical Learning Periods Awareness*. DeFL highlights the negligence of the impact of underlying deep neural networks in the existing byzantine-robust defenses. Authors define critical learning periods (CLP) as the first training rounds in the FL cycle. They propose a CLP-aware poisoning defense in FL. DeFL measures the fine-grained differences between DNN model updates by calculating the federated gradient norm vector (FGNV) metric. DeFL uses FGNV to identify CLP and detect the presence of malicious clients. Authors claim this technique to be robust against model poisoning attacks and detection errors.

CLP is important because a model's performance depends on the training quality in the first few rounds. Poor model training may result in irreversible model degradation despite high-quality training in later rounds. However, calculating CLP incurs a huge cost, like the eigenvalues of the Hessian. The authors propose a novel, easy-to-compute metric to identify CLP.

5.8.1 Federated Gradient Norm Vector (FGNV)

Considering a deep neural network model with L layers, the difference in the model update for a client i on layer j evaluated on sample ξ is $\Delta \ell_i^j = \ell \left(\mathbf{w}_i^j - \eta g_i \left(\mathbf{w}_i^j; \xi \right); \xi \right) - \ell \left(\mathbf{w}_i^j; \xi \right)$, which can be approximated using Taylor expansion as stated in Equation 5.6.

$$\Delta \ell_i^j \approx -\eta \left\| g_i \left(\mathbf{w}_i^j; \xi \right) \right\|^2 \tag{5.6}$$

This is called as FGNV of client i on layer j, i.e., $\text{FGNV}_i^j :=$ $\Delta\ell_i^j$. Then, FGNV of round t on layer j is the weighted average of FGNV of all clients, i.e.,

$$\text{FGNV}^j(t) = \sum_{i \in \mathcal{N}(t)} \frac{|\mathcal{D}_i|}{\sum_{i \in \mathcal{N}(t)} |\mathcal{D}_i|} \text{FGNV}_i^j(t) \qquad (5.7)$$

5.8.2 Detecting Malicious Clients

Given FGNV^j, compute $\hat{\beta}_{i'} = \frac{\text{Cov}\left(\mathbf{FGNV}_i^j, \text{FGNV}_{i'}^j\right)}{\text{Var}\left(\text{FGNV}_{i'}^j\right)}$. Then, find an index of client i on layer j as follows:

$$I\left(\text{FGNV}_i^j, \mathbf{FGNV}^j\right) = \frac{1}{|\mathcal{N}(t)|} \sum_{i'=1}^{|\mathcal{N}(t)|} \hat{\beta}_{i'} \qquad (5.8)$$

The layer j is marked as outlier if it deviates significantly from others. Then, they design a simple voting mechanism to determine the malicious participants.

Further, the authors designed a threshold-based rule to identify CLP based on FGNV as follows:

$$\frac{\sum_{j=1}^{L} \text{FGNV}^j(t) - \sum_{j=1}^{L} \text{FGNV}^j(t-1)}{\sum_{j=1}^{L} \text{FGNV}^j(t-1)} \geq \delta \qquad (5.9)$$

where δ is the defined threshold. Once CLP is identified, the weights of all malicious clients are set to 0. To protect honest clients from getting falsely detected as malicious, a Bayesian model estimates the probability of givingng good updates. In a round t, the probability (weight) score calculated for client i is defined below.

$$p_i(t) = \frac{\alpha_i(t)}{\alpha_i(t) + \beta_i(t)} \qquad (5.10)$$

where α_i and β_i are initialized at the start of the FL cycle. Next, $\alpha_i(t) = \alpha_i(t-1)$ if the client is honest in round t else $\beta_i(t) = \beta_i(t-1)$.

5.8.3 Evaluation

Authors evaluated non-identically an independent distributed(non-IID) FL scenario. They considered the adversary's knowledge Full and Partial and simulated against state-of-the-art model poisoning attacks in [6, 18, 60]. DeFl proved to be 12.04× more effective against these attacks than the best-performing defenses. They also evaluated the sensitivity of the threshold (δ) and the impact of non-IID degrees. With increasing δ in {0, 0.05, 0.2, 0.35, 0.5}, fewer rounds are marked in CLP, and global model accuracy is not significantly impacted. They set $\delta = 0.5$ unless stated otherwise. DeFL (global model) performance is increased with decreasing degree of non-IID. This is expected because decreasing the degree of heterogeneity causes easy detection of adversaries.

5.9 RDFL

RDFL [66] is a robust defense algorithm to mitigate backdoor attacks in FL. RDFL consists of four components: (1) picking eligible parameters for calculating cosine similarity among local model updates; (2) adaptive clustering; (3) detecting suspicious models; and (4) adaptive clipping.

RDFL makes the following assumptions: (1) There exists a partitioning of clients in the presence of malicious clients, such that every subset of clients satisfies the conventional FL system. (2) There is a high similarity between two malicious updates compared to the similarity between two benign ones.

Top k parameters: A deep neural network model has millions of parameters, but all of them are not important; some of them are redundant. Parameter indices with high absolute values are important in each local model update. Parameters at the union of all parameter indices are considered important parameters.

5.9.1 Adaptive Clustering

Authors in [10, 58] used hierarchical clustering in non-IID FL without considering malicious participants. Poisoning impacts the performance of hierarchical clustering. Authors in [53] used a density-based clustering algorithm, HDBSCAN, to solve the above issue, assuming the majority of honest participants. However, HDBSCAN fails when all the malicious participants send the same local model update. It fails only in the presence of 20% attackers. This is because HDBSCAN removes honest updates due to the non-IID scenario and the high similarity of malicious updates.

RDFL combines hierarchical clustering with HDBSCAN for adaptive clustering. To execute hierarchical clustering, RDFL uses a cosine similarity-based distance metric ($\mathcal{T}$), such that $\mathcal{T}_{ij} = \sum(\mathcal{H}_i - \mathcal{H}_j)^2$, where $\mathcal{H}_{ij} = 1 - \frac{\left\langle \Delta w^{i'}, \Delta w^{j'} \right\rangle}{\|\Delta w^{i'}\|\|\Delta w^{j'}\|}$. RDFL first executes HDBSCAN on $\mathcal{T}$. Under an honest scenario or weak heterogeneity, most participants will be clustered in the same groups and may be considered outliers. Thus, RDFL presents multiple thresholds. If the number of outliers exceeds a threshold ($len(\mathcal{T}) \times \beta_1$), all clients are considered for aggregation, where authors considered $\beta_1 = 0.8$. Under a non-IID scenario, where most benign clients are removed as outliers, RDFL uses hierarchical clustering if the number of outliers exceeds a threshold ($len(\mathcal{T}) \times \beta_2$), where authors considered $\beta_2 = 0.4$.

5.9.2 Detecting Malicious Models

Now, RDFL has to choose the cluster with honest participants. RDFL calculates the cosine distance of each cluster as $\mathcal{P}_c = \text{Median}(\text{Median}_{i \in c}(\mathcal{H}_{ci}))$, where c is the cluster and $\mathcal{H}_{ci}$ is the cosine similarity vector for each client i to other clients in the cluster c. The median is robust, assuming that more than half of the participants are honest. Now, based on the second assumption, $\mathcal{P}_c > \mathcal{P}_{c'}$, where c and c' are for benign and malicious clusters, respectively. The cluster with a minimum value of $\mathcal{P}_c$ is selected for aggregation.

Existing byzantine-robust defenses rely on similarity-based methods to detect outliers among the local model updates. The majority of the defenses can be categorized into two types: (1) target estimation of the true optimal model center using robust mean and median operations; (2) by designing anomaly-detection methods by training/calibrating extra (supplementary) information. The first category of defense is limited to the assumption of a homogeneous data distribution, while the second category requires additional information. Further, these techniques have limitations: (1) the number of malicious clients; (2) work only with access to a validation dataset with the central server; (3) ignore the impact of underlying DNN.

5.10 FLTC: FL TRUSTED COORDINATES

Based on existing attacks and defenses, we can draw the following points:

- Byzantine participants can maintain both high and low cosine similarity with two benign updates. This increases the number of supporters for malicious updates and opponents for benign updates [6].

- Byzantine participants can manipulate Euclidean distance-based aggregation rules. Sybils support each other and help themselves get selected by moving the center [8].

- Among the existing baseline defenses, coordinate-level aggregation rules like Median and Trimmed-Mean [74] are more resistant to poisoning attacks.

FLTC [37] is a Byzantine-robust defense performing coordinate-wise aggregation by bootstrapping root trust at the central server. An aggregator gets the trusted base update by training over a small, clean dataset. In order to train, the aggregator only needs a small clean dataset so that the samples can be manually collected and labeled. A participant's local update is compared to the trusted base update using direction cosine, which measures the change in direction and magnitude between the two. It is possible, however, for coordinates on both sides of the reference update to achieve high similarity. FLTC addresses this using a majority-based approach.

5.10.1 Trusted Coordinates

FLTC uses hyper spherical direction cosine to assign trust score (φ_i^k) to each coordinate k of local model update (w_i) of client i, based on the change in direction and magnitude with respect to server base update (∇_{BS}), as stated below:

$$\varphi_i^k = \frac{\nabla_{BS}^k - \nabla w_i^k}{\sqrt{\sum_{k=1}^d (\nabla w_i^k - \nabla_{BS}^k)^2}}, \tag{5.11}$$

for each $k \in [d]$ dimension. After that, FLTC finds the number of coordinates with positive and negative direction cosines and selects the majority of those. Then, min-max normalization is performed over the selected trusted coordinates, and zero scores are assigned to the remaining untrusted coordinates.

Finally, the central server does the weighted average of the local model updates, as stated below:

$$\nabla w^k = \sum_{i=1}^n \frac{\varphi_i^k}{\sum_{j=1}^n \varphi_j^k} \nabla w_i^k. \tag{5.12}$$

5.10.2 Adaptive Attack

Given that, the system has m (out of n) malicious clients. Considering malicious clients, the global model can be written as,

$$\nabla w^{k'} = \sum_{i=1}^{m} \frac{\varphi_i^k}{\sum_{j=1}^{m} \varphi_j^k + \sum_{j=m+1}^{n} \varphi_j^k} \nabla w_i^{k'}$$
$$+ \sum_{i=m+1}^{n} \frac{\varphi_i^k}{\sum_{j=1}^{m} \varphi_j^k + \sum_{j=m+1}^{n} \varphi_j^k} \nabla w_i^k. \tag{5.13}$$

Local Model Poisoning Attack Framework: Authors in [18] formulated the local model poisoning attack framework as an optimization problem.

$$\max_{\nabla w_1', \nabla w_2', \cdots, \nabla w_m'} s^T \left(\nabla w - \nabla w' \right),$$
$$\text{subject to } \nabla w = \mathcal{A} \left(\nabla w_1, \cdots, \nabla w_m, \nabla w_{m+1}, \nabla w_n \right).$$
$$\nabla w' = \mathcal{A} \left(\nabla w_1', \cdots, \nabla w_m', \nabla w_{m+1}, \nabla w_n \right).$$
$$\tag{5.14}$$

The column vector s represents the sign (direction) of the before-attack global model ∇w. An attacker designs model updates in the reverse direction of what would happen if /nablaw were to change. Specifically, it reduces to solving $\nabla w - \lambda s$ for evaluating λ.

FLTC assigns trust scores to the coordinates of all local model updates. Suppose φ is the $n \times d$ trust score matrix with n number of participants and each local model update with d coordinates. Then, s can be computed as $[\text{sgn}(\varphi_i^1), \text{sgn}(\varphi_i^2), \ldots, \text{sgn}(\varphi_i^k)]_{i \in n}$, where $k \in [d]$. sgn is based on the majority of the sign of φ_i^k for the local model updates before attack.

Further, an optimization function is solved as $\nabla_{BS} - \lambda s$ for λ, based on the above-discussed framework. If $s_j = -1$, the malicious j^{th} coordinate is sampled in the interval $[\nabla_{BS}^j,$

$b.\nabla_{BS}^{j}]$ (when $\nabla_{BS}^{j} > 0$) or $[\nabla_{BS}^{j}, \nabla_{BS}^{j}/b]$ (when $\nabla_{BS}^{j} \leq 0$), otherwise, it is sampled in the interval $[\nabla_{BS}^{j}/b, \nabla_{BS}^{j}]$ (when $\nabla_{BS}^{j} > 0$) or $[b.\nabla_{BS}^{j}, \nabla_{BS}^{j}]$ (when $\nabla_{BS}^{j} \leq 0$). As in trim attack, the attack does not depend on b; it is set as 2.

5.10.3 Evaluation

Based on the results reported, the attack impact is bounded by 0.5% for MNIST, around 0.5% for Fashion-MNIST, and by 2% for CIFAR-10, considering 20% malicious participants, while the attack impact is bounded by 1% for MNIST and Fashion-MNIST, and around 2.5% for CIFAR-10, considering 40% malicious participants. The attack impact is bounded by 2% for MNIST and Fashion-MNIST and by 3% for CIFAR-10, considering 40% attackers, against adaptive attack settings.

5.11 IMPLEMENTATION

5.11.1 FoolsGold

```
def FoolsGold(base_model, models, **kwargs):
    len_grad = len(sim.get_net_arr(base_model)
        [0])
    model_list = list(models.values())
    n_clients = len(model_list)

    grads = np.zeros((n_clients, len_grad))
    for index, model in enumerate(model_list):
        grads[index] = sim.get_net_arr(model)
            [0]

    cs = smp.cosine_similarity(grads) - np.eye(
        n_clients)
    maxcs = np.max(cs, axis=1)

    # pardoning
    for i in range(n_clients):
        for j in range(n_clients):
            if i == j:
                continue
            if maxcs[i] < maxcs[j]:
```

```
19              cs[i][j] = cs[i][j] * maxcs[i]
                    / maxcs[j]
20          wv = 1 - (np.max(cs, axis=1))
21          wv[wv > 1] = 1
22          wv[wv < 0] = 0
23
24          # Rescale so that max value is wv
25          wv = wv / np.max(wv)
26          wv[(wv == 1)] = .99
27
28          # Logit function
29          wv = (np.log(wv / (1 - wv)) + 0.5)
30          wv[(np.isinf(wv) + wv > 1)] = 1
31          wv[(wv < 0)] = 0
32
33          updated_model_list = []
34          for index, model in enumerate(model_list):
35              model = scale_model(model, wv[index])
36              updated_model_list.append(model)
37
38          model = reduce(add_model,
                  updated_model_list)
39          model = scale_model(model, 1.0 / len(models
                  ))
40          if base_model is not None:
41              model = sub_model(base_model, model)
42          return model
```

5.11.2 FLTrust

```
1   def FLTrust(base_model, models, **kwargs):
2       base_model_update = kwargs["
            base_model_update"]
3       base_norm = kwargs["base_norm"] if "
            base_norm" in kwargs else True
4
5       if base_norm:
6           # Base Model Norm
7           base_model_update_norm = sim.grad_norm(
                base_model_update)
8
```

```
model_list = list(models.values())
ts_score_list=[]
fl_score_list=[]
updated_model_list = []
for model in model_list:
    ts_score = sim.grad_cosine_similarity(
        base_model_update, model)

    # Relu
    if ts_score < 0:
        ts_score = 0
    ts_score_list.append(ts_score)

    if base_norm:
        # Model Norm
        norm = sim.grad_norm(model)
        ndiv = base_model_update_norm/norm
        scale_norm = ts_score * ndiv
        model = scale_model(model,
            scale_norm)
        fl_score_list.append(scale_norm)
    else:
        model = scale_model(model, ts_score
            )

    updated_model_list.append(model)

log.info("Cosine Score {}".format(
    ts_score_list))
log.info("FLTrust Score {}".format(
    fl_score_list))

model = reduce(add_model,
    updated_model_list)
model = scale_model(model, 1.0 / sum(
    ts_score_list))

if base_model is not None:
    model = sub_model(base_model, model)
return model
```

5.11.3 Krum

```
def Krum(base_model, models, **kwargs):
    model_list = list(models.values())
    model_keys = list(models.keys())

    beta = kwargs["beta"]
    lb = beta//2
    ub = len(model_list) - beta//2 - 1

    euclidean_dists = []
    for index1, model1 in enumerate(model_
    list):
        model_dists = []
        for index2, model2 in enumerate(
            model_list):
            if index1 != index2:
                dist = sim.grad_eucliden_dist(
                    model1, model2)
                model_dists.append(dist)
        sq_dists = torch.sum(torch.sort(torch.
            tensor(model_dists)).values[lb:ub])
        euclidean_dists.append(sq_dists)

    min_model_index = euclidean_dists.index(min
        (euclidean_dists))
    log.info("Krum Candidate is {}".format(
        model_keys[min_model_index]))

    model = model_list[min_model_index]
    if base_model is not None:
        model = sub_model(base_model,
            model_list[min_model_index])
    return model
```

5.11.4 Multi-Krum

```
def M_Krum(base_model, models, **kwargs):
    model_list = list(models.values())
    model_keys = list(models.keys())

    beta = kwargs['beta"]
    lb = beta//2
    ub = len(model_list) - beta//2 - 1

    euclidean_dists = []
    for index1, model1 in enumerate(model_list)
        :
        model_dists = []
        for index2, model2 in enumerate(
            model_list):
            if index1 != index2:
                dist = sim.grad_eucliden_dist(
                    model1, model2)
                model_dists.append(dist)
        sq_dists = torch.sum(torch.sort(torch.
            tensor(model_dists)).values[lb:ub])
        euclidean_dists.append(sq_dists)

    min_model_indices = np.argpartition(np.
        array(euclidean_dists), len(model_list)
        - 2*beta - 2)
    min_model_indices = min_model_indices[:len(
        model_list) - 2*beta - 2]
    log.info("M_Krum Candidates are {}".format
        ([model_keys[index] for index in
        min_model_indices]))

    model_list = [model for index, model in
        enumerate(model_list) if index in
        min_model_indices]

    model = reduce(add_model, model_list)
    model = scale_model(model, 1.0 / len(models
        ))
```

```
27
28    if base_model is not None:
29        model = sub_model(base_model, model)
30    return model
```

5.11.5 Median

```
1    def Median(base_model, models, **kwargs):
2        model_list = list(models.values())
3        dummy_model = model_list[0]
4        dummy_model_arr, d_list = sim.get_net_arr(
             dummy_model)
5
6        beta = kwargs["beta"]
7        lb = beta
8        ub = len(model_list) - beta
9
10       updated_model_list = []
11       for model in model_list:
12           model_arr, _ = sim.get_net_arr(model)
13           updated_model_list.append(model_arr)
14
15       updated_model_tensors = torch.tensor(
             updated_model_list)
16       merged_updated_model_tensors = torch.sort(
             torch.stack([model for model in
             updated_model_tensors], 0), dim = 0)
17       merged_updated_model_arrs = torch.transpose
             (merged_updated_model_tensors.values, 0,
             1).numpy()
18       merged_updated_model_indices = torch.
             transpose(merged_updated_model_tensors.
             indices, 0, 1).numpy()
19
20       model_arr = np.zeros(len(dummy_model_arr))
21       for index, arr in enumerate(
             merged_updated_model_arrs):
22           model_arr[index] = np.median(arr)
23       model = sim.get_arr_net(dummy_model,
             model_arr, d_list)
24
```

```
if base_model is not None:
    model = sub_model(base_model, model)
return model
```

5.11.6 Trimmed-Mean

```
def T_Mean(base_model, models, **kwargs):
    model_list = list(models.values())
    dummy_model = model_list[0]
    dummy_model_arr, d_list = sim.get_net_arr(
        dummy_model)

    beta = kwargs["beta"]
    lb = beta
    ub = len(model_list) - beta

    updated_model_list = []
    for model in model_list:
        model_arr, _ = sim.get_net_arr(model)
        updated_model_list.append(model_arr)

    updated_model_tensors = torch.tensor(
        updated_model_list)
    merged_updated_model_tensors = torch.sort(
        torch.stack([model for model in
        updated_model_tensors], 0), dim = 0)
    merged_updated_model_arrs = torch.transpose
        (merged_updated_model_tensors.values, 0,
        1).numpy()

    model_arr = np.zeros(len(dummy_model_arr))
    for index, arr in enumerate(
        merged_updated_model_arrs):
        model_arr[index] = arr[lb:ub].mean(0)
    model = sim.get_arr_net(dummy_model,
        model_arr, d_list)

    if base_model is not None:
        model = sub_model(base_model, model)
    return model
```

5.11.7 DnC

```
def DnC(base_model, models, **kwargs):
    num_buckets=1
    bucket=100000
    all_updates = []
    _list = None

    for model in list(models.values()):
        model_arr, _list = sim.get_net_arr(
            model)
        all_updates.append(model_arr)

    all_updates = torch.tensor(all_updates)
    n, d = all_updates.shape

    n_attackers = kwargs["beta"]

    final_indices = []

    for p in np.arange(num_buckets):
        idx = np.sort(np.random.choice(d,
            bucket, replace=False))
        sampled_all_updates = all_updates[:,
            idx]
        sampled_good_updates = all_updates[
            n_attackers:][:, idx]

        centered_all_updates =
            sampled_all_updates - torch.mean(
            sampled_all_updates, 0)
        centered_good_updates =
            sampled_good_updates - torch.mean(
            sampled_good_updates, 0)

        u, s, v = torch.svd(
            centered_all_updates)
        u_g, s_g, v_g = torch.svd(
            centered_good_updates)

        scores = torch.mm(centered_all_updates,
            v[:,0][:, None]).cpu().numpy()
```

```
        final_indices.append(list(np.argsort(
            scores[:,0]**2)[:(n-int(1.5*
            n_attackers))])))

    result = set(final_indices[0])
    for currSet in final_indices[1:]:
        result.intersection_update(currSet)
    final_idx = np.array(list(result))
    # print(np.array(final_idx), len((final_idx
        )))

    model = sim.get_arr_net(base_model, torch.
        mean(all_updates[final_idx], 0).numpy(),
        _list)

    if base_model is not None:
        model = sub_model(base_model, model)
    return model
```

## CHAPTER 6

Privacy-Preserving FL

THERE IS A CRITICAL need for secure and inference-resistant aggregation mechanisms in Federated Learning (FL) due to the presence of potentially curious or semi-honest servers and participants, especially when operating over unauthenticated or untrusted communication networks. The local model updates exchanged during the training process can still leak sensitive information about the users' private data. An adversary, including the central server or even other collaborating clients, may attempt to infer properties of the training data or reconstruct individual records by observing these updates. To address these risks, various privacy-preserving aggregation mechanisms have been proposed, which aim to ensure that local data remain private even in the presence of such inference attempts. In this chapter, we explore established privacy enhancing technologies (PETs) tailored to FL, including differential privacy (DP), secure multiparty computation (SMPC), and homomorphic encryption (HE). We discuss their design principles, strengths, limitations, and practical deployment considerations in FL.

DOI: 10.1201/9781003688570-6

6.1 DIFFERENTIAL PRIVACY

Differential Privacy (DP) is a mathematical framework for estimating the computational dependence of a given output to any of the input data points [16]. According to Cynthia Dwork, Differential Privacy describes a data holder's promise to a data subject. The subject should not be affected, adversely or otherwise, by allowing the data to be used in any study or analysis, no matter what other studies, datasets, or information sources are available. The presence or absence of a given data point should not make significant changes to any computation. For any two datasets D_1 and D_2 having only one data point not in common, the given output O over computation f is said to be providing (ϵ, δ)-differential privacy if,

$$\Pr\left(\{(D_1) \in O\right) \leq e^\epsilon \Pr\left(\{(D_2) \in O\right) + \delta \qquad (6.1)$$

The computation is said to satisfy ϵ-differential privacy given $\delta = 0$. Differential Privacy can be achieved by adding noise to each data point or directly to the output over the data points. The amount of sensitivity is calculated based on the maximum difference in the output with the exclusion of a data point. The noise added is calculated based on sensitivity. The parameter ϵ controls the tradeoff between the accuracy of the differentially private f and the information it leaks. Gaussian and Laplacian noises are the most common mechanisms for adding distortion to obscure sensitive information. However, it involves a tradeoff between accuracy and privacy. Round-level differential privacy protects from membership inference attacks but remains vulnerable to property inference attacks. Participant-level differential privacy achieves optimal error for loss minimization using SGD and is a suitable approach to deal with property inference attacks.

6.1.1 DPFL: A Client-Level Perspective

Authors in [23] proposed a Differentially Private Federated Learning (DPFL) protocol emphasizing client-level DP. The proposed protocol aims to ensure clients' privacy without degrading the performance. Especially with a high number of participants, it achieved privacy with a negligible drop in accuracy. The sum of local models is distorted using the Gaussian mechanism. The sensitivity (S) is enforced using scaled versions, such that the second norm of any update is bounded by S, i.e., $||\Delta w||_2 < S$. Each model update (Δw) can be scaled/visualized as $\frac{\Delta w}{max(1, \frac{||\Delta w||_2}{S})}$. While aggregation, the central server adds noise (scaled to S) to the sum of local model updates. Choosing S is strategic, as it should be small to limit the noise variance, and originality should also be maintained for the accuracy of the learning process. Based on the study in [1], it is selected as the median of the norm of all the local model updates. However, the median may be a source of potential leakage.

6.2 HOMOMORPHIC ENCRYPTION

Homomorphic encryption (HE) [73] is a form of encryption that allows computations to be performed on encrypted data without first decrypting it. It enables mathematical operations over encrypted data, producing an encrypted result that can be decrypted to the same value as if the operation was performed on unencrypted data. This enables computations to be performed on sensitive data while preserving its confidentiality. Formally, homomorphic encryption can be defined as follows.

Let E be an encryption function that inputs a plaintext message m and a public key pk, producing a ciphertext c as output. Let D be a decryption function that takes a ciphertext c and a private key sk as input and produces a plaintext message m as output. Let f be a function that takes two plaintext messages x and y as input and produces a plaintext message z as output, such that $z = f(x, y)$. The homomorphic encryption of f is a function that takes as input two ciphertexts $c1 = E(x, pk)$ and $c2 = E(y, pk)$ and produces as output a ciphertext $c3 = E(z, pk)$, such that $D(c3, sk) = z$.

Homomorphic encryption has numerous applications in finance, healthcare, and cloud computing, where sensitive data needs to be processed without compromising privacy [77]. For example, it can perform secure computations on medical data without revealing any patient information or enable secure cloud computing where the cloud provider cannot access the data being processed. One of the main challenges of homomorphic encryption is that it can be computationally expensive, making it less practical for certain applications.

6.2.1 BatchCrypt: HE-Based Scheme

Authors in [77] proposed BatchCrypt, a homomorphic encryption (HE)-based improvement tailored to FL. Authors have used FATE[1] as the FL framework, which has built-in support for the Paillier (additive homomorphic encryption) cryptosystem. Batchcrypt is also designed to support other partially HE cryptosystems. It proposed novel quantization and encoding schemes with a gradient clipping scheme. Thus, it encodes a batch of quantized gradients into a long integer. It achieved $23\times-93\times$ improvement in training time and $66\times-101\times$ reduction in the communication overhead. Still, it maintains accuracy with a negligible drop. In the encrypted domain, time taken in training for Fashion-MNIST, CIFAR, and LSTM models is 211.9 s, 2725.7 s, and 8777.7 s, which are $96\times$, $135\times$, and $154\times$ compared to the plaintext. Also, the data communication for Fashion-MNIST, CIFAR, and LSTM models are 1.1 GB, 13.1 GB, and 44.1 GB in the encrypted domain, compared to 6.98 MB, 85.89 MB, and 275.93 MB

---

[1] https://fate.fedai.org/

in the plaintext. In the complete training process, 60% of the time is spent on encrypting the local model update, 20% on decrypting it, and the remaining 20% on communication. A large exponent and modulus (usually larger than 512 bits) are required for encryption and decryption operations, making them extremely computationally expensive. When using additively HE, like Paillier, the ciphertext size is roughly the same as the key size, regardless of the plaintext size. Since the minimum secure key size in 2019 is 2048, a gradient is a 32-bit floating point number, so the size already translates to 64× after inflation. Paillier only encrypts integers, so floating-point values have to be scaled beforehand. Additionally, their exponent information contributes more to data inflation. To address such issues, authors discuss various solutions, such as specialized FGPA accelerating encryption by 3×. However, it will not be useful to reduce the communication overhead. Thus, the intuition is to reduce the volume of data for encryption. Batchcrypt performed batching over gradients to form a long plaintext. In order to maintain the additive property, authors proposed quantization to convert gradient values to signed integers uniformly distributed in a symmetric range. This scheme adopts two's complement representation, with two signed bits for quantized values.

6.2.2 Threshold Multi-Key HE Scheme

In the above scheme, all clients are supposed to use the same public-private key pair. Thus, there exists a privacy risk; each client can read the gradient update of any other client. Also, only one client can collude with the server to decrypt all the other updates. Thus, authors in [14] proposed a threshold multi-key HE scheme (tMK-CKKS), which addresses such collusion attacks. It is resistant to collusion between the server and t clients. This means that clients require at least t to decrypt. This work is an improvement over a multi-key homomorphic encryption-based scheme (xMK-CKKS), which requires all the clients to decrypt. Thus, authors claim to achieve 1.21× improved computation speed over xMK-CKKS and 15.84× over Batchcrypt. They used the FedML[2] framework for implementation. In this scheme, the public key used for encryption is accessible to all the clients. Secret keys are generated based on a linear secret-sharing scheme, requiring at least t clients for decryption. As it is based on fully homomorphic encryption, its security depends on ring learning with errors, which can be considered post-quantum security.

6.3 SECURE MULTI-PARTY COMPUTATION

Secure Multi-Party Computation (SMPC) is a cryptographic approach where different parties wish to jointly calculate an arbitrary function while revealing no one's contribution to the output. It was first introduced for two parties (2PC) by Yao et al. [72] and got extended for multiple parties (MPC). It aims for privacy, independence, and fairness to the contributors. Formally, SMPC can be defined as follows.

Let F be a function that takes n inputs, denoted as $F(x_1, x_2, ..., x_n)$. Let $P_1, P_2, ..., P_n$ be n parties, each with their own private input x_i. Secure multi-party computing aims to enable these parties to jointly compute the function F without revealing their private inputs to each other while ensuring the computation's correctness and preserving the input's privacy.

In SMPC, the parties collaborate to perform the computation while keeping their inputs secret. They use cryptographic techniques, such as encryption and secret sharing, to ensure their inputs remain private. SMPCs are used in a wide range of applications, including data analysis, voting systems, and financial transactions, where multiple parties need to collaborate while protecting their privacy and maintaining the integrity of the computation.

---

[2] https://www.fedml.ai/

Though SMPC secures the process, it may reveal sensitive information from the output. It is less computationally intensive compared to homomorphic encryption-based protocols. However, it incurs high communication overhead. Secure aggregation protocol is its variant proposed by Google [9]. It suffers from high latency due to multiple communications needed to average the local gradients securely. It is also susceptible to Sybil attack, with the majority of computation done by colluded participants. The authors proposed single- and double-masking protocols in [69], which describes how to protect user privacy and verify the integrity of aggregated results from the server by using a variant of secret sharing technology that handles participants going offline or dropping out in-between.

6.3.1 Practical Secure Aggregation

This protocol [9] is designed to enable multiple parties to collectively train a machine learning model without revealing their data. This approach utilizes a combination of homomorphic encryption and secret-sharing techniques to ensure that the data remains private throughout the aggregation process. The authors demonstrate the effectiveness of their protocol through experiments on real-world datasets, showing that it can provide strong privacy guarantees while maintaining high accuracy in the resulting model.

6.3.1.1 Intuition

The goal is to aggregate the local model updates of multiple users so that the server only learns a share of any user's local model update and finally outputs the sum of all the local model updates.

6.3.1.2 Masking with One-time Pads

Assuming users (u, v) with an order $u < v$, and they agree on a common random vector $s_{u,v}$. The intuition behind this is that if u adds $s_{u,v}$ and v subtracts $s_{u,v}$ from their respective local model update, then $s_{u,v}$ will be canceled out.

Thus, each user encrypts its local model update (x_u) as stated below:

$$y_u = x_u + \sum_{v \in \mathcal{U}:u<v} s_{u,v} - \sum_{v \in \mathcal{U}:u>v} s_{v,u} (\mathrm{mod}\,R), \qquad (6.2)$$

and shares y_u to the server.

Then, the server aggregates as stated below:

$$\begin{aligned} z &= \sum_{u \in \mathcal{U}} y_u \\ &= \sum_{u \in \mathcal{U}} \left(x_u + \sum_{v \in \mathcal{U}:u<v} s_{u,v} - \sum_{v \in \mathcal{U}:u>v} s_{v,u} \right). \qquad (6.3) \\ &= \sum_{u \in \mathcal{U}} x_u \quad (\mathrm{mod}\,R) \end{aligned}$$

However, this approach has certain drawbacks in that it incurs heavy communication overheads to establish pairwise random vectors. Also, it has no mechanism to handle users dropping out.

6.3.1.3 Efficient Communication and Handling of Dropped Users

Users agree on common seeds for a pseudorandom number generator (PRG) using Diffie-Hellman public keys, despite the commonly agreed vector $(s_{u,v})$.

A threshold secret sharing scheme can be used to handle dropped-out users, and the shares of Diffie-Hellman public key are shared with all other users. If any user drops out, their key can be reconstructed by remaining (at least t) users.

However, this approach also has drawbacks in that the server may receive any user's update late and reconstruct the user's key by then. Then, the server can learn the user's plaintext update.

6.3.1.4 Double Masking

To mitigate the issue of unmasking updates of dropped-out users by the server, each user samples another random seed b_u. User generates shares of $s_{u,v}$ and b_u and compute encrypted update as stated below:

$$
\begin{aligned}
y_u = x_u + \; & \text{PRG} \; (b_u) \\
+ \; & \sum_{v \in \mathcal{U}:u<v} \text{PRG} \left(s_{u,v} \right) \\
- \; & \sum_{v \in \mathcal{U}:u>v} \text{PRG} \left(s_{v,u} \right) \quad (\bmod R)
\end{aligned}
\tag{6.4}
$$

In the case of a dropped-out user, the server has to request a share of $s_{u,v}$ or b_u as any honest user will not share both shares with the server. If at least t honest users exist, the server cannot decrypt the local model update of any user.

6.3.1.5 Methodology

Each participant knows the security parameter k, total number of participants n, a threshold value t, honestly generated $pp \to KA.gen(k)$, input sample space $\mathbb{Z}_R^m$ with parameters m and R, and a field $\mathbb{F}$ for secret sharing. KA stands for key agreement. Each participant also has a private communication channel with the central server.

Each participant receives a secret key d_u^{SK} from the trusted third party and a public (verification) key d_v^{PK} associated with each remaining participant v.

6.3.1.5.1 Round 0 Each participant generates key pairs $(c_u^{PK}, c_u^{SK}) \leftarrow \mathbf{KA} \cdot \text{gen}(pp), (s_u^{PK}, s_u^{SK}) \leftarrow \mathbf{KA} \cdot \mathbf{gen}(pp)$ and $\sigma_u \leftarrow \text{SIG} \cdot \text{sign} \left(d_u^{SK}, c_u^{PK} \| s_u^{PK} \right)$. A standard UF-CMA secure signature scheme (SIG $.gen$, SIG $.sign$, SIG $.ver$) is used. Then, each participant sends $(c_u^{PK}, s_u^{PK} \| \sigma_u^{PK})$ to the server through a secure communication channel.

The server collects at least t messages from individual participants, and this set of participants is referred to as $\mathcal{U}_1$. Otherwise, the server aborts the FL cycle. Then, the server broadcasts $\{(v, c_v^{PK}, s_v^{PK}, \sigma_v)\}_{v \in \mathcal{U}_1}$.

6.3.1.5.2 Round 1 Each participant receives $\{(v, c_v^{PK}, s_v^{PK}, \sigma_v)\}_{v \in \mathcal{U}_1}$, then verifies (1) $|\mathcal{U}_1| \geq t$; (2) each public key pair is different; (3) $\forall v \in \mathcal{U}_1$, SIG.ver $(d_v^{PK}, c_v^{PK} \| s_v^{PK}, \sigma_u) = 1$.

Then, the participant does the following: (1) samples a random element $b_u \to \mathbb{F}$, which is to be used as a seed for Pseudorandom Number Generator (PRG); (2) generates t (out of $|\mathcal{U}_1|$) shares of s_u^{SK} : $\{(v, s_{u,v}^{SK})\}_{v \in \mathcal{U}_1} \leftarrow$ SS.share $(s_u^{SK}, t, \mathcal{U}_1)$; (3) generates t (out of $|\mathcal{U}_1|$) shares of b_u : $\{(v, b_{u,v})\}_{v \in \mathcal{U}_1} \leftarrow$ SS.share $(b_u, t, \mathcal{U}_1)$; (4) computes $e_{u,v} \leftarrow$ AE.enc(KA.agree $(c_u^{SK}, c_v^{PK}), u \| v \| s_{u,v}^{SK} \| b_{u,v})$, for each participant $v \in \mathcal{U}_1 \backslash \{u\}$; (5) abort if any of the above operation fails; (6) submits all $e_{u,v}$ to the server; (7) stores all the received messages and generated values in this round.

Further, the server collects the list of ciphertexts from at least t (out of $|\mathcal{U}_1|$) participants, denoted as $\mathcal{U}_2$. Then, the server sends $\{e_{u,v}\}_{v \in \mathcal{U}_2}$ to each other participant.

6.3.1.5.3 Round 2 Each user receives $\{e_{u,v}\}_{v \in \mathcal{U}_2}$ from the server and verifies that the size of the list of received ciphertexts is at least t. Otherwise, aborts.

Then, user u computes $s_{u,v} \leftarrow$ KA.agree (s_u^{SK}, s_v^{PK}) and finds $p_{u,v} \leftarrow \Delta_{u,v}.\text{PRG}(s_{u,v})$, where $\Delta_{u,v} = 1$ if $u > v$, else $\Delta_{u,v} = -1$, such that $p_{u,v} + p_{v,u} = 0, \forall u \neq v$. Also, define $p_{u,u} = 0$.

Further, each user computes its private mask $p_u = \text{PRG}(b_u)$ and masks the input vector as: $y_u \leftarrow x_u + p_u + \sum_{v \in \mathcal{U}_2} p_{u,v} (mod R)$. Then, each user sends y_u to the server.

The server collects y_u from at least t users, and this set of the participants is referred to as $\mathcal{U}_3$.

6.3.1.5.4 Round 3 Each user receives $\mathcal{U}_3$, consisting of at least t users (including user itself). Then the user sends $\sigma'_u \leftarrow$ SIG.sign$(d_u, \mathcal{U}_3)$ to the server.

Further, the server collects σ'_u from at least t users, and this set of participants is referred to as $\mathcal{U}_4$. And, the server sends to each user in $\mathcal{U}_4$ the set $\{v, \sigma'_v\}_{v \in \mathcal{U}_4}$.

6.3.1.5.5 Round 4 Each user receives $\{v, \sigma'_v\}_{v \in \mathcal{U}_4}$ and verifies that

SIG.ver$(d^{PK}, \mathcal{U}_3, \sigma'_v) = 1, \forall v \in \mathcal{U}_4$.

For users $v \in \mathcal{U}_2 \backslash \{u\}$, each user decrypts ciphertexts as:

$v' \| u' \| s^{SK}_{v,u} \| b_{v,u} \leftarrow$ **AE.dec** (KA.agree $(c^{SK}_u, c^{PK}_v), e_{v,u}$),

received in round 2, and asserts $u = u'$ and $v = v'$. Also, the user sends list of shares consisting of $s^{SK}_{v,u}$ for users $v \in \mathcal{U}_2 \backslash \mathcal{U}_3$ and $b_{v,u}$ for users in $v \in \mathcal{U}_3$.

Then, the server receives responses from at least t users, and this set of participants is referred to as $\mathcal{U}_5$. For each user $u \in \mathcal{U}_2 \backslash \mathcal{U}_3$, the server reconstructs $s^{SK}_u \leftarrow$ SS. recon $\left(\left\{ s^{SK}_{u,v} \right\}_{v \in \mathcal{U}_5}, t \right)$, to recompute $p_{u,v} \forall v \in \mathcal{U}_3$ using PRG. Similarly, the server reconstructs $b_u \leftarrow$ SS. recon $\left(\left\{ b_{u,v} \right\}_{v \in \mathcal{U}_5}, t \right)$ to recompute p_u using PRG.

Finally, the server aggregates as: $z = \sum_{u \in \mathcal{U}_3} x_u$ as $\sum_{u \in \mathcal{U}_3} x_u = \sum_{u \in \mathcal{U}_3} y_u - \sum_{u \in \mathcal{U}_3} p_u + \sum_{u \in \mathcal{U}_3, v \in \mathcal{U}_2 \backslash \mathcal{U}_3} p_{v,u}$.

Table 6.1 summarizes the techniques used in privacy-preserving FL over different factors, including overheads, scalability, security level, and use cases.

TABLE 6.1 Comparison between Different Privacy Enhancing Technologies

Technique	Guarantee	Overhead	Scalability Level	Weaknesses	Use Cases
Differential Privacy	Formal mathematical guarantees (via noise addition)	Low to Moderate	High Moderate	Accuracy privacy tradeoff, privacy loss over time	Healthcare, finance, IoT data
SMPC	Strong privacy (secure function evaluation)	High	Low to Moderate Strong	High computational and communication cost	Sensitive data (government, medical research)
Homomorphic Encryption	Strong encryption guarantees (computation on encrypted data)	Very High	Low Very Strong	Computationally expensive, slower processing	Financial applications, highly sensitive datasets
Secure Aggregation	Privacy via encrypted updates and aggregation	Moderate	High Strong	Does not defend against adversarial updates	Large-scale FL, mobile applications
Trusted Execution Environments	Hardware-based isolation for computations	Low to Moderate	Low to Moderate Strong	Hardware-specific vulnerabilities, limited scalability	Cloud-based federated learning, secure hardware setups

6.4 IMPLEMENTATION

6.4.1 Differential Privacy

```python
import torch
import numpy as np

def clip_by_l2_norm(update, max_norm):
    """
    Clips the update to have L2 norm at most
        max_norm.
    """
    norm = torch.norm(update)
    if norm > max_norm:
        update = update * (max_norm / norm)
    return update


def add_gaussian_noise(aggregated_update,
    sensitivity, noise_multiplier, device='cpu')
    :
    """
    Adds Gaussian noise to the aggregated
        update.
    """
    noise = torch.normal(
        mean=0.0,
        std=noise_multiplier * sensitivity,
        size=aggregated_update.shape,
        device=device
    )
    return aggregated_update + noise


def dp_aggregate(updates, sensitivity,
    noise_multiplier):
    """
    Clips each update, aggregates them, and
        adds DP noise.
    """
    clipped_updates = []
    for update in updates:
```

```
          clipped = clip_by_l2_norm(update,
              sensitivity)
          clipped_updates.append(clipped)

      summed_update = torch.stack(clipped_updates
          ).sum(dim=0)
      noisy_update = add_gaussian_noise(
          summed_update, sensitivity,
          noise_multiplier)

      return noisy_update / len(updates)

# === Example Usage ===

# Suppose each client returns a model update
num_clients = 50
update_dim = 10000
device = 'cuda' if torch.cuda.is_available()
    else 'cpu'

# Randomly generated updates for illustration
local_updates = [torch.randn(update_dim, device
    =device) for _ in range(num_clients)]

# Select S as median of L2 norms
l2_norms = torch.tensor([torch.norm(update).
    item() for update in local_updates])
sensitivity = torch.median(l2_norms).item()

# Noise multiplier for privacy guarantee (ε, δ)
noise_multiplier = 1.0  # You would choose this
    based on desired (ε, δ)

# Aggregate updates with DP
dp_global_update = dp_aggregate(local_updates,
    sensitivity, noise_multiplier)

# Apply update to global model (assuming `
    global_model` is a flattened tensor)
# global_model += dp_global_update
```

6.4.2 Homomorphic Encryption

```
import tenseal as ts

def ckks_context():
    context = ts.context(ts.SCHEME_TYPE.CKKS,
        8192, coeff_mod_bit_sizes=[60,40,40,60])
    #context = ts.context(ts.SCHEME_TYPE.CKKS,
        16384, coeff_mod_bit_sizes=[31, 26, 26,
        26, 26, 26, 26, 26, 26, 26, 31])
    context.global_scale = pow(2, 40)
    return context

context = ckks_context()
context.generate_galois_keys()

p_context = context.serialize(save_public_key=
    False, save_secret_key=False,
    save_galois_keys=False, save_relin_keys=
    False)

import base64

def writeCkks(ckks_vec, filename):
    ser_ckks_vec = base64.b64encode(ckks_vec)

    with open(filename, 'wb') as f:
        f.write(ser_ckks_vec)

def readCkks(filename):
    with open(filename, 'rb') as f:
        ser_ckks_vec = f.read()

    return base64.b64decode(ser_ckks_vec)


arr, slist = get_net_arr(model)#[0:8000]
print(len(arr))

import pickle
with open('plain_model.pkl','wb') as f:
    pickle.dump(arr, f)
```

```
start = time.time()
enc_ckks_model = ts.ckks_vector(context, arr)
enc_ckks_model_ser = enc_ckks_model.serialize()
writeCkks(enc_ckks_model_ser, "enc_model")
print(time.time()-start)
print(len(arr))
```

6.4.3 Practical Secure Aggregation

We are giving an example that mimics practical secure aggregation. It can be implemented as it is using cryptographic protocols.

```
import torch
import random

def generate_mask(seed, dim):
    """
    Deterministically generate a mask using a
        shared seed.
    """
    generator = torch.Generator()
    generator.manual_seed(seed)
    return torch.randn(dim, generator=generator
        )

def mask_update(local_update, shared_seeds,
    client_id, total_clients, dim):
    """
    Applies pairwise masks to the local update.
    Each client generates a mask with every
        other client and masks accordingly.
    """
    masked_update = local_update.clone()

    for other_id in range(total_clients):
        if other_id == client_id:
            continue
        seed = shared_seeds[min(client_id,
            other_id)][max(client_id, other_id)]
        mask = generate_mask(seed, dim)
        if client_id < other_id:
```

```
                masked_update += mask   # send mask
            else:
                masked_update -= mask   # receive
                    mask
        return masked_update



# === Example Simulation ===
num_clients = 4
update_dim = 10000
device = 'cuda' if torch.cuda.is_available()
    else 'cpu'



# Each client creates a local update
local_updates = [torch.randn(update_dim, device
    =device) for _ in range(num_clients)]


# Step 1: Simulate pairwise shared seeds
shared_seeds = {
    i: {j: random.randint(0, 1e6) for j in
        range(i+1, num_clients)}
    for i in range(num_clients)
}



# Step 2: Each client masks their update
masked_updates = []
for client_id in range(num_clients):
    masked = mask_update(local_updates[
        client_id], shared_seeds, client_id,
        num_clients, update_dim)
    masked_updates.append(masked)



# Step 3: Server aggregates masked updates
aggregated_masked = torch.stack(masked_updates)
    .sum(dim=0)

```

```
# Result: Server gets the correct sum of all
    local updates (masks cancel out)
true_sum = torch.stack(local_updates).sum(dim
    =0)
error = torch.norm(aggregated_masked - true_sum
    )
print(f"Error in aggregation (should be near
    zero): {error.item()}")
```

Bibliography

[1] Martin Abadi, Andy Chu, Ian Goodfellow, H. Brendan McMahan, Ilya Mironov, Kunal Talwar, and Li Zhang. Deep learning with differential privacy. In *Proceedings of the 2016 ACM SIGSAC conference on computer and communications security*, Vienna, Austria, pages 308–318, 2016.

[2] Alham Fikri Aji and Kenneth Heafield. Sparse communication for distributed gradient descent. *arXiv preprint arXiv:1704.05021*, 2017. https://doi.org/10.48550/arXiv.1704.05021

[3] Sana Awan, Bo Luo, and Fengjun Li. Contra: Defending against poisoning attacks in federated learning. In Elisa Bertino, Haya Shulman, and Michael Waidner (Eds.), *European symposium on research in computer security*, pages 455–475. Springer, 2021.

[4] Eugene Bagdasaryan, Andreas Veit, Yiqing Hua, Deborah Estrin, and Vitaly Shmatikov. How to backdoor federated learning. In Silvia Chiappa and Roberto Calandra, editors, *Proceedings of the twenty third international conference on artificial intelligence and statistics, volume 108 of proceedings of machine learning research*, pages 2938–2948. PMLR, 26–28 August 2020.

[5] Eugene Bagdasaryan, Andreas Veit, Yiqing Hua, Deborah Estrin, and Vitaly Shmatikov. How to backdoor federated learning. In *International conference on artificial intelligence and statistics*, Palermo, Sicily, Italy, pages 2938–2948. PMLR, 2020.

[6] Gilad Baruch, Moran Baruch, and Yoav Goldberg. A little is enough: Circumventing defenses for distributed learning. In H. Wallach, H. Larochelle, A. Beygelzimer, F. d'Alché-Buc,

E. Fox, and R. Garnett (Eds.), *Neural information processing systems*. Curran Associates, Inc., 2019.

[7] Battista Biggio, Luca Didaci, Giorgio Fumera, and Fabio Roli. Poisoning attacks to compromise face templates. In *2013 international conference on biometrics (ICB)*, Madrid, Spain, pages 1–7. IEEE, 2013.

[8] Peva Blanchard, El Mahdi El Mhamdi, Rachid Guerraoui, and Julien Stainer. Machine learning with adversaries: Byzantine tolerant gradient descent. In I. Guyon, U. V. Luxburg, S. Bengio, H. Wallach, R. Fergus, S. Vishwanathan, and R. Garnett (Eds.), *Advances in neural information processing systems*. Curran Associates, Inc., 2017.

[9] Keith Bonawitz, Vladimir Ivanov, Ben Kreuter, Antonio Marcedone, H. Brendan McMahan, Sarvar Patel, Daniel Ramage, Aaron Segal, and Karn Seth. Practical secure aggregation for privacy-preserving machine learning. In *Proceedings of the 2017 ACM SIGSAC conference on computer and communications security, CCS '17*, New York, NY, USA, pages 1175-1191, Association for Computing Machinery, 2017.

[10] Christopher Briggs, Zhong Fan, and Peter Andras. Federated learning with hierarchical clustering of local updates to improve training on non-IID data. In *2020 international joint conference on neural networks (IJCNN)*, Glasgow, United Kingdom, pages 1–9, 2020.

[11] Xiaoyu Cao, Minghong Fang, Jia Liu, and Neil Zhenqiang Gong. Fltrust: Byzantine-robust federated learning via trust bootstrapping. *arXiv preprint arXiv:2012.13995*, 2021. https://doi.org/10.48550/arXiv.2012.13995

[12] Xiaoyu Cao and Neil Zhenqiang Gong. Mpaf: Model poisoning attacks to federated learning based on fake clients. In *Proceedings of the IEEE/CVF conference on computer vision and pattern recognition*, New Orleans, LA, USA, pages 3396–3404, 2022.

[13] Koby Crammer, Alex Kulesza, and Mark Dredze. Adaptive regularization of weight vectors. In Yoshua Bengio, Dale Schuurmans, John D. Lafferty, Christopher K. I. Williams, and Aron Culotta (Eds.), *Advances in Neural Information Processing Systems*, 22, pages 414–422. Curran Associates, Inc., 2009.

[14] Weidong Du, Min Li, Liqiang Wu, Yiliang Han, Tanping Zhou, and Xiaoyuan Yang. A efficient and robust privacy-preserving framework for cross-device federated learning. *Complex & Intelligent Systems*, 9, pages 1–15, 2023.

[15] Cynthia Dwork. Differential privacy. In Michele Bugliesi, Bart Preneel, Vladimiro Sassone, and Ingo Wegener (Eds.), *International colloquium on automata, languages, and programming*, pages 1–12. Springer Berlin Heidelberg, Series: Lecture Notes in Computer Science, Vol. 4052, 2006.

[16] Cynthia Dwork. Differential privacy in new settings. In *Proceedings of the twenty-first annual ACM-SIAM symposium on discrete algorithms*, Austin, Texas, USA, pages 174–183. SIAM, 2010.

[17] European Commission. Regulation (EU) 2016/679 of the European Parliament and of the Council of 27 April 2016 on the protection of natural persons with regard to the processing of personal data and on the free movement of such data, and repealing Directive 95/46/EC (General Data Protection Regulation) (Text with EEA relevance), 2016.

[18] Minghong Fang, Xiaoyu Cao, Jinyuan Jia, and Neil Gong. Local model poisoning attacks to byzantine-robust federated learning. In *29th USENIX security symposium (USENIX security 20)*, Boston, MA, USA, pages 1605–1622, 2020.

[19] Matt Fredrikson, Somesh Jha, and Thomas Ristenpart. Model inversion attacks that exploit confidence information and basic countermeasures. In *Proceedings of the 22nd ACM SIGSAC conference on computer and communications security*, Denver, Colorado, USA, pages 1322–1333, 2015.

[20] Clement Fung, Chris J.M. Yoon, and Ivan Beschastnikh. Mitigating sybils in federated learning poisoning. *arXiv preprint arXiv:1808.04866*, 2018. https://doi.org/10.48550/arXiv.1808.04866

[21] Clement Fung, Chris J.M. Yoon, and Ivan Beschastnikh. The limitations of federated learning in sybil settings. In *23rd International symposium on research in attacks, intrusions and defenses (RAID 2020)*, San Sebastian, Spain, pages 301–316, 2020.

[22] Jonas Geiping, Hartmut Bauermeister, Hannah Dröge, and Michael Moeller. Inverting gradients-how easy is it to break privacy in federated learning? *Advances in Neural Information Processing Systems*, 33:16937–16947, 2020.

[23] Robin C. Geyer, Tassilo Klein, and Moin Nabi. Differentially private federated learning: A client level perspective. *arXiv preprint arXiv:1712.07557*, 2017. https://doi.org/10.48550/arXiv.1712.07557

[24] Amirata Ghorbani and James Y. Zou. Neuron shapley: Discovering the responsible neurons. *Advances in Neural Information Processing Systems*, 33:5922–5932, 2020.

[25] Ian Goodfellow, Jean Pouget-Abadie, Mehdi Mirza, Bing Xu, David Warde-Farley, Sherjil Ozair, Aaron Courville, and Yoshua Bengio. Generative adversarial nets. In Z. Ghahramani, M. Welling, C. Cortes, N. D. Lawrence, and K. Q. Weinberger (Eds.), *Advances in neural information processing systems*, Montréal, Québec, Canada. Curran Associates, Inc., 2014.

[26] Rachid Guerraoui, Sébastien Rouault, et al. The hidden vulnerability of distributed learning in byzantium. In *International conference on machine learning*, Stockholm, Sweden, pages 3521–3530. PMLR, 2018.

[27] Baoru Han, Rutvij Jhaveri, Han Wang, Dawei Qiao, and Jinglong Du. Application of robust zero-watermarking scheme based on federated learning for securing the healthcare data. *IEEE Journal of Biomedical and Health Informatics*, 27(2):804–813, 2021.

[28] Meng Hao, Hongwei Li, Xizhao Luo, Guowen Xu, Haomiao Yang, and Sen Liu. Efficient and privacy-enhanced federated learning for industrial artificial intelligence. *IEEE Transactions on Industrial Informatics*, 16(10):6532–6542, 2019.

[29] Andrew Hard, Kanishka Rao, Rajiv Mathews, Swaroop Ramaswamy, Françoise Beaufays, Sean Augenstein, Hubert Eichner, Chloé Kiddon, and Daniel Ramage. Federated learning for mobile keyboard prediction. *arXiv preprint arXiv:1811.03604*, 2018. https://doi.org/10.48550/arXiv.1811.03604

[30] Briland Hitaj, Giuseppe Ateniese, and Fernando Perez-Cruz. Deep models under the gan: Information leakage from collaborative deep learning. In *Proceedings of the 2017 ACM SIGSAC conference on computer and communications security*, Dallas, Texas, USA, pages 603–618, 2017.

[31] Yangsibo Huang, Samyak Gupta, Zhao Song, Kai Li, and Sanjeev Arora. Evaluating gradient inversion attacks and

defenses in federated learning. *Advances in Neural Information Processing Systems*, 34:7232–7241, 2021.

[32] Matthew Jagielski, Alina Oprea, Battista Biggio, Chang Liu, Cristina Nita-Rotaru, and Bo Li. Manipulating machine learning: Poisoning attacks and countermeasures for regression learning. In *2018 IEEE symposium on security and privacy (SP)*, San Francisco, CA, USA, pages 19–35. IEEE, 2018.

[33] Xiao Jin, Pin-Yu Chen, Chia-Yi Hsu, Chia-Mu Yu, and Tianyi Chen. Cafe: Catastrophic data leakage in vertical federated learning. *Advances in Neural Information Processing Systems*, 34:994–1006, 2021.

[34] Pentti Kanerva. Hyperdimensional computing: An introduction to computing in distributed representation with high-dimensional random vectors. *Cognitive Computation*, 1(2):139–159, 2009.

[35] Harsh Kasyap and Somanath Tripathy. Hidden vulnerabilities in cosine similarity based poisoning defense. In *2022 56th annual conference on information sciences and systems (CISS)*, Princeton University, Princeton, NJ, US, pages 263–268. IEEE, 2022.

[36] Harsh Kasyap and Somanath Tripathy. Beyond data poisoning in federated learning. *Expert Systems with Applications*, 235:121192, 2024.

[37] Harsh Kasyap and Somanath Tripathy. Sine: Similarity is not enough for mitigating local model poisoning attacks in federated learning. *IEEE Transactions on Dependable and Secure Computing*, 21(5):4481–4494, 2024.

[38] Xiangjie Kong, Haoran Gao, Guojiang Shen, Gaohui Duan, and Sajal K Das. Fedvcp: A federated-learning-based cooperative positioning scheme for social internet of vehicles. *IEEE Transactions on Computational Social Systems*, 9(1):197–206, 2021.

[39] Parth Parag Kulkarni, Harsh Kasyap, and Somanath Tripathy. Dnet: An efficient privacy-preserving distributed learning framework for healthcare systems. In *International conference on distributed computing and internet technology*, Bhubaneswar, Odisha, India, pages 145–159. Springer, 2021.

[40] Yann LeCun, Corinna Cortes, and C.J. Burges. Mnist handwritten digit database. Available: http://yann. lecun. com/exdb/mnist, 1998.

[41] Xingyu Li, Zhe Qu, Shangqing Zhao, Bo Tang, Zhuo Lu, and Yao Liu. Lomar: A local defense against poisoning attack on

federated learning. *IEEE Transactions on Dependable and Secure Computing*, 20(1):437–450, 2021.

[42] Tao Lin, Lingjing Kong, Sebastian U. Stich, and Martin Jaggi. Ensemble distillation for robust model fusion in federated learning *Advances in Neural Information Processing Systems*, 33:2351–2363, 2020.

[43] Yang Liu, Yan Kang, Chaoping Xing, Tianjian Chen, and Qiang Yang. A secure federated transfer learning framework. *IEEE Intelligent Systems*, 35(4):70–82, 2020.

[44] Yingqi Liu, Shiqing Ma, Yousra Aafer, Wen-Chuan Lee, Juan Zhai, Weihang Wang, and Xiangyu Zhang. Trojaning attack on neural networks. In *Network and distributed systems security (NDSS) symposium 2018*, San Diego, CA, USA, 18–21 February 2018.

[45] Guodong Long, Yue Tan, Jing Jiang, and Chengqi Zhang. Federated learning for open banking. In Qiang Yang, Lixin Fan, and Han Yu (Eds.), *Federated learning: privacy and incentive*, pages 240–254. Springer, 2020.

[46] Xinjian Luo, Yuncheng Wu, Xiaokui Xiao, and Beng Chin Ooi. Feature inference attack on model predictions in vertical federated learning. In *2021 IEEE 37th international conference on data engineering (ICDE)*, Chania, Crete, Greece, pages 181–192. IEEE, 2021.

[47] Arpan Manna, Harsh Kasyap, and Somanath Tripathy. Moat: model agnostic defense against targeted poisoning attacks in federated learning. In *Information and communications security: 23rd international conference, ICICS 2021, Chongqing, China, November 19–21, 2021, Proceedings, Part I 23*, pages 38–55. Springer, 2021.

[48] Debasmita Manna, Harsh Kasyap, and Somanath Tripathy. Milsa: Model interpretation based label sniffing attack in federated learning. In *International conference on information systems security*, IIT Tirupati, Tirupati, India, pages 139–154. Springer, 2022.

[49] Yunlong Mao, Xinyu Yuan, Xinyang Zhao, and Sheng Zhong. Romoa: Robust model aggregation for the resistance of federated learning to model poisoning attacks. In *European symposium on research in computer security*, Darmstadt, Germany, pages 473–496. Springer, 2021.

[50] Brendan Mcmahan, Eider Moore, Daniel Ramage, Seth Hampson, and Blaise Aguera y Arcas. Communication-efficient learning of deep networks from decentralized data. In Aarti Singh and Jerry Zhu (Eds.), *Artificial intelligence and statistics*, pages 1273–1282. PMLR, 2017.

[51] H. Brendan Mcmahan, Eider Moore, Daniel Ramage, and Blaise Agüera y Arcas. Federated learning of deep networks using model averaging. *CoRR*, 2016. https://doi.org/10.48550/arXiv.1602.05629

[52] Milad Nasr, Reza Shokri, and Amir Houmansadr. Comprehensive privacy analysis of deep learning: Passive and active white-box inference attacks against centralized and federated learning. In *2019 IEEE symposium on security and privacy (SP)*, San Francisco, CA, USA, pages 739–753. IEEE, 2019.

[53] Thien Duc Nguyen, Phillip Rieger, Roberta De Viti, Huili Chen, Björn B Brandenburg, Hossein Yalame, Helen Möllering, Hossein Fereidooni, Samuel Marchal, Markus Miettinen, et al. {FLAME}: Taming backdoors in federated learning. In *31st USENIX security symposium (USENIX security 22)*, Boston, MA, USA, pages 1415–1432, 2022.

[54] Junjie Pang, Yan Huang, Zhenzhen Xie, Qilong Han, and Zhipeng Cai. Realizing the heterogeneity: A self-organized federated learning framework for iot. *IEEE Internet of Things Journal*, 8(5):3088–3098, 2020.

[55] Ahmed Salem, Yang Zhang, Mathias Humbert, Pascal Berrang, Mario Fritz, and Michael Backes. Ml-leaks: Model and data independent membership inference attacks and defenses on machine learning models. *arXiv preprint arXiv:1806.01246*, 2019. https://doi.org/10.48550/arXiv.1806.01246

[56] Tim Salimans, Ian Goodfellow, Wojciech Zaremba, Vicki Cheung, Alec Radford, and Xi Chen. Improved techniques for training gans. In D. D. Lee, M. Sugiyama, U. V. Luxburg, I. Guyon, and R. Garnett (Eds.), *Advances in neural information processing systems*, Barcelona, Spain. Curran Associates, Inc., 2016.

[57] Iqbal H. Sarker. Machine learning: Algorithms, real-world applications and research directions. *SN Computer Science*, 2(3):160, 2021.

[58] Felix Sattler, Klaus-Robert Müller, and Wojciech Samek. Clustered federated learning: Model-agnostic distributed

multitask optimization under privacy constraints. *IEEE Transactions on Neural Networks and Learning Systems*, 32(8):3710–3722, 2020.

[59] Thomas Schneider. Practical secure function evaluation. In *Informatiktage*, Gesellschaft für Informatik (GI), as part of the Informatiktage Congress publications, LNI series, Bonn, Germany, pages 37–40, 2008.

[60] Virat Shejwalkar and Amir Houmansadr. Manipulating the byzantine: Optimizing model poisoning attacks and defenses for federated learning. In *NDSS*, The Internet Society, Virtual mode, page 1278, 2021.

[61] Reza Shokri, Marco Stronati, Congzheng Song, and Vitaly Shmatikov. Membership inference attacks against machine learning models. In *IEEE symposium on security and privacy*, San Jose, CA, USA, pages 3–18. IEEE, 2017.

[62] Narendra Singh, Harsh Kasyap, and Somanath Tripathy. Collaborative learning based effective malware detection system. In *Joint European conference on machine learning and knowledge discovery in databases*, Ghent, Belgium, pages 205–219. Springer, 2020.

[63] Vale Tolpegin, Stacey Truex, Mehmet Emre Gursoy, and Ling Liu. Data poisoning attacks against federated learning systems. In *European symposium on research in computer security*, Guildford, United Kingdom, pages 480–501. Springer International Publishing, 2020.

[64] Hongyi Wang, Kartik Sreenivasan, Shashank Rajput, Harit Vishwakarma, Saurabh Agarwal, Jy-yong Sohn, Kangwook Lee, and Dimitris Papailiopoulos. Attack of the tails: Yes, you really can backdoor federated learning. *Advances in Neural Information Processing Systems*, 33:16070–16084, 2020.

[65] Lixu Wang, Shichao Xu, Xiao Wang, and Qi Zhu. Eavesdrop the composition proportion of training labels in federated learning. *arXiv preprint arXiv:1910.06044*, 2019. https://doi.org/10.48550/arXiv.1910.06044

[66] Yongkang Wang, Di-Hua Zhai, Yongping He, and Yuanqing Xia. An adaptive robust defending algorithm against backdoor attacks in federated learning. *Future Generation Computer Systems*, 143:118–131, 2023.

[67] Zhibo Wang, Mengkai Song, Zhifei Zhang, Yang Song, Qian Wang, and Hairong Qi. Beyond inferring class representatives: User-level privacy leakage from federated learning.

In *IEEE INFOCOM 2019-IEEE conference on computer communications*, Paris, France, pages 2512–2520. IEEE, 2019.

[68] Kang Wei, Jun Li, Ming Ding, Chuan Ma, Howard H Yang, Farhad Farokhi, Shi Jin, Tony QS Quek, and H Vincent Poor. Federated learning with differential privacy: Algorithms and performance analysis. *IEEE Transactions on Information Forensics and Security*, 15:3454–3469, 2020.

[69] Guowen Xu, Hongwei Li, Sen Liu, Kan Yang, and Xiaodong Lin. Verifynet: Secure and verifiable federated learning. *IEEE Transactions on Information Forensics and Security*, 15:911–926, 2019.

[70] Gang Yan, Hao Wang, Xu Yuan, and Jian Li. Defl: Defending against model poisoning attacks in federated learning via critical learning periods awareness. In *Proceedings of the AAAI conference on artificial intelligence*, Washington, D.C., USA, pages 10711–10719, 2023.

[71] Haibo Yang, Xin Zhang, Minghong Fang, and Jia Liu. Byzantine-resilient stochastic gradient descent for distributed learning: A lipschitz-inspired coordinate-wise median approach. In *2019 IEEE 58th conference on decision and control (CDC)*, Nice, France, pages 5832–5837. IEEE, 2019.

[72] Andrew Chi-Chih Yao. How to generate and exchange secrets. In *27th annual symposium on foundations of computer science (sfcs 1986)*, Toronto, Ontario, Canada, pages 162–167. IEEE, 1986.

[73] Xun Yi, Russell Paulet, Elisa Bertino, Xun Yi, Russell Paulet, and Elisa Bertino. *Homomorphic encryption*. Springer, 2014.

[74] Dong Yin, Yudong Chen, Ramchandran Kannan, and Peter Bartlett. Byzantine-robust distributed learning: Towards optimal statistical rates. In *International conference on machine learning*, Stockholm, Sweden, pages 5650–5659. PMLR, 2018.

[75] Dong Yin, Yudong Chen, Kannan Ramchandran, and Peter Bartlett. Byzantine-robust distributed learning: Towards optimal statistical rates. In *International conference on machine learning*, Stockholm, Sweden, pages 5650–5659, 2018.

[76] Kai Yue, Richeng Jin, Chau-Wai Wong, Dror Baron, and Huaiyu Dai. Gradient obfuscation gives a false sense of

security in federated learning. In *32nd USENIX security symposium (USENIX security 23)*, Anaheim, CA, USA, pages 6381–6398, 2023.

[77] Chengliang Zhang, Suyi Li, Junzhe Xia, Wei Wang, Feng Yan, and Yang Liu. Batchcrypt: Efficient homomorphic encryption for cross-silo federated learning. In *Proceedings of the 2020 USENIX annual technical conference (USENIX ATC 2020)*, Boston, MA, USA, 2020.

[78] Jiale Zhang, Junjun Chen, Di Wu, Bing Chen, and Shui Yu. Poisoning attack in federated learning using generative adversarial nets. In *2019 18th IEEE international conference on trust, security and privacy in computing and communications/13th IEEE international conference on big data science and engineering (TrustCom/BigDataSE)*, Rotorua, New Zealand, pages 374–380. IEEE, 2019.

[79] Jingwen Zhang, Jiale Zhang, Junjun Chen, and Shui Yu. Gan enhanced membership inference: A passive local attack in federated learning. In *ICC 2020 - 2020 IEEE international conference on communications (ICC)*, pages 1–6, Dublin, Ireland, 2020.

[80] Zhe Zhang, Shiyao Ma, Zhaohui Yang, Zehui Xiong, Jiawen Kang, Yi Wu, Kejia Zhang, and Dusit Niyato. Robust semi-supervised federated learning for images automatic recognition in internet of drones. *IEEE Internet of Things Journal*, 10(7):5733–5746, 2022.

[81] Zhi-Hua Zhou. *Machine learning*. Springer Nature, 2021.

[82] Ligeng Zhu, Zhijian Liu, and Song Han. Deep leakage from gradients. In Z. Ghahramani, M. Welling, C. Cortes, N. D. Lawrence, and K. Q. Weinberger (Eds.), *Advances in neural information processing systems*, pages 14747–14756. Curran Associates, Inc., 2019.

Index